JOY and
in HIS SERVICE

True stories from the mission field
By ALENE DALLEY

AuthorHouse™
1663 Liberty Drive
Bloomington, IN 47403
www.authorhouse.com
Phone: 1-800-839-8640

First published by AuthorHouse 05/04/2009

ISBN: 1-9781-4389-5027-3 (sc)
1-9781-4389-5026-6 (hc)

Printed in the United States of America
Bloomington, Indiana

This book is printed on acid-free paper.

JOY AND ADVENTURE IN HIS SERVICE

By Alene Dalley

Dedicated to God the Father

Jesus, my Lord and Savior

To God's Holy Spirit

An Ordinary Person's Mission From God

There are many different types of mission trips. There are also many different kinds of accommodations. For those of you who are not as adventurous or like the comforts of home, there are mission trips for you, too. The following stories are true experiences on the mission field. I pray that you will enjoy reading them as much as I enjoyed living them.

Alene Dalley

Thank you to some very special dedicated missionaries and mission organizations. Without them, my mission work would not have happened.   Innovative Missions Opportunities

Global Missions Fellowship & E-Partners

International Commissions

Mike Downey

To my very special friends I met and worked with on the mission field.

Mike Jorghenson

Joel Reeves

Jewel Gruer

Jeannie Tidwell

Jerry Squyres

Ajay Torres

I extend appreciation to my wonderful friends Betty Walden, Nadyne Carlisle, Carolyn Jones, Melba Hall, Joy Pitts and Frances Richardson who have all helped me immensely in fulfilling my mission from God, and especially to Joy and Carolyn for being open to God who worked through them to get me where He wanted me...in the mission field.

God gave special Christian friendships.

Jewel Gruer and Alene Dalley

Jeannie Tidwell and Alene Dalley

We met on a mission trip and became friends. We went on many mission trips together as roommates. We are friends forever.

There are some countries we go into where we are not welcome by the local government. I will tell you some stories from these countries but I will not name the country and, as in all my mission trips, I will change the names of the people so that they will not have repercussions from their government or even their families. In some countries, if a person receives Christ he will be disowned or even killed. Stories are from the following countries:

Mexico

Guatemala

Venezuela

Nicaragua

Peru

Belarus

Romania

Kosovo

Israel

Cameroon, Africa

Zambia, Africa

India

Taiwan

Columbia

TABLE OF CONTENTS

THE LONG ROAD TO WHERE GOD COULD USE ME

In 1985 I was 47 years old. I had started working for a financial organization in 1958 when I was 21 years old. There had been a lot of broken service due to the birth of my children, but I had had a working relationship now for 27 years. In 1958 I started working as a teller and when I left the company, I was vice-president of a nine billion dollar institution. I had a great job, great people to work for, a good salary, but suddenly everything seemed to start going wrong. The individual who owned the company sold it and new people came in with new ideas. This was about the third new owner and about the fourth computer conversion since I had been there, but this time it was different for me. There was no problem with my staying, I had the job, but I had been feeling for a year that God wanted something else of me. The job made me miserably ill. My husband and I talked it over and decided I would retire. On October 1, 1985, I gave my notice and my superior couldn't believe it. I stayed on until January 1986.

1986 was a traumatic year. My elderly widowed Mother was very ill and an aunt was going through a hard time. They constantly needed me, but they were all in Oklahoma while I lived in Texas. To top it off, my best friend found she had cancer with only a few months to live. I was needed and available whenever they asked me.

Then came June 11, 1987, a date I will never forget. I was sitting under my hairdryer reading <u>Combat Faith</u> by Hal Lindsey. I closed my eyes. I tried several times to open them, but I could not. The following words came into my head.

"Your eyes have been opened unto the Word of the Lord. You will follow in the paths I will lead."

When I was able to open my eyes, I felt so relaxed, almost as if I had taken a tranquilizer. I felt at peace. Obviously God was trying to tell me He wanted something of me.

My friend died July 5, 1987. Shortly after, another friend called and invited me to go with a group of ladies from work to Mexico for a vacation. I told her I had no desire to go to Mexico. I had already been to Mexico many times.

I knew God wanted something of me. Finally, one day I said, "I give up, God. I don't know what You want me to do, but if You will make known to me what You want so that I know it is Your will and not mine, I will do it. Open the door and I will go through it." That same week I ran into Carolyn Jones, a lady I had known years before. We both currently went to Sagemont Church. We decided we would take our granddaughters to the Houston zoo. As Carolyn was getting out of the car, she said, "Alene, do you remember Rose who used to be in our church?" I told her I knew the name but I had never met her. Carolyn said, "She is going to Mexico City on a mission trip." It is hard to describe how I felt, but in that moment, I knew what God wanted me to do. We went into the zoo with our two granddaughters and I said nothing to Carolyn.

Alene Dalley

Carolyn Jones

When I returned home that evening, I called Rose and left a message on her recorder. "My name is Alene Dalley from Sagemont Baptist Church. I understand you are going on a mission trip to Mexico City. I am interested in going. Will you call me back? I need information."

Rose called so excited, she said she had been praying for a woman to go with her to be her roommate. I went to Rose's house to meet her for the first time. The next day I called our church and went down to the mission pastor's office, Dr. Hal Boone. Sagemont Baptist Church was very large, so Dr. Boone did not know me. He quizzed me thoroughly, then started telling me the reasons I could not go. First, I didn't know the Spanish language; secondly, I needed a passport. I told him I had signed up that morning for a crash course in Spanish, and that I already had a passport. When I finished, he smiled at me and said, "I believe you are going on a mission trip." He was just trying to make sure it was God calling me since he did not personally know me. Then he started helping me to prepare myself with scripture to assist me on my first mission trip for God. I left the church and drove to Carolyn's house. When I told Carolyn all that had happened

4

she was speechless. She was amazed that God had used her to open the door for me to serve as a short term missionary.

A few days later, I was stopped at a red light five blocks from my house. While waiting for the light to change, I did not hear a voice, but heard words in my head, "You can't go on this mission trip, you can't quote scriptures well enough, you don't have the money, and you can't leave your husband." These words then came to me, "You will do nothing. The Holy Spirit will do it all." I drove the five blocks home and my husband met me at the back door. He said, "Alene, I know you have been worried about the money for this mission trip, but if you feel this is what you are supposed to do, don't worry. We will find the money." This was on Thursday. The next Sunday we went to church where my pastor John Morgan preached, "If God wants you to do something for Him, don't worry about those you leave behind, because God will take care of them." I was in a daze, in awe that God wanted me to do this and Satan had attacked me with three doubts. But God had answered all three doubts. I knew I was supposed to go on this mission trip to Mexico City and I had promised God I would go if He would open the door.

5

Three weeks after I first heard about the mission trip, I was in Mexico City on a mission for God. Me, Alene Dalley, a nobody, not a preacher nor a teacher! But I was who God wanted – a child of God, saved by the blood of Jesus Christ. I had told God I wasn't worthy, but I was willing. That is all God needs – a willing Christian for Him to do His work through.

INTRODUCTION TO A MISSION DAY

We landed in Mexico City. I don't know the language so I just follow the leader. We go through immigration. "Have your passports and visas ready." Well, that wasn't so bad. Now we pick up our luggage. Boy, am I ever glad I tied a bright colored ribbon to my luggage or I would never have found it. Now it is time for customs. "Push the button." If it is green you go on your way; if it is red, you go to the table and the officials go through your luggage. Whew, I don't have to go through that this time, but what about next time? "Okay, everybody put your luggage on the bus and climb on, for we will be at the hotel in about forty-five minutes."

There is the hotel. Well, it doesn't look like I expected, but I'm sure it will be fine. "Everybody off the bus and wait, for we have to check in as a group." And we wait, and wait, and wait. Well, everything is in God's timing. "Alene, you will be in room 305 and your roommate is Rose." Rose and I meet each other for the first time and get our luggage. Where is the elevator? NO ELEVATOR! We finally get our luggage to the third floor and collapse onto the bed.

This is my first trip as a short term missionary. How did I get here? It all happened so fast! I don't know anybody! Well, I have found where I sleep. What do I eat? What do I do? God, are you sure this is where you want me?

Relax and enjoy! You are only going to be here for one week. Wait on the Lord, Alene, and see what He has in store for you.

We meet our teammates and are assigned to a new territory where a local church would like to start a new mission work. Tomorrow morning at 9:00 A.M. we will meet our Mexican teammates.

Good morning! It is time for a Prayer Breakfast. Everyone is smiling, though a little hesitant wondering how the day will go. "Everybody get a plate and go to the buffet, then have a chair, for it is time to start our morning off with the Lord!" First, we have prayer, and then we dig into this delicious Mexican breakfast. Before I am finished, someone picks up his guitar and the singing starts, praising our God. Wow, is this wonderful with all the different voices, denominations and nationalities. This must be a little like what heaven will be like.

Breakfast is over and the nationals are here to meet us and take us out for the day's work. Here I come, Lord. I don't know how You can use such as me, but I am Yours, for whatever You want, just use me according to Your purpose and to Your glory.

BALLOONS FOR GOD

We have gone out to our area to do door to door witnessing. It is market day and no one is at home. The streets are closed to traffic and booths are set up for blocks. Booths of anything you can think of…fruit, vegetables, clothes, toys…line the streets. We decided we would write on the tracks about the church service that night at the home of the future pastor. My Mexican teammate was a medical doctor. I told him I could make animal balloons and the children could write in Spanish the time and the address on the balloons. The children were excited and had fun writing on the balloons. Then we took them to the market place and gave them away. While I was walking through the market with the doctor ahead of me, a little brown hand grabbed my arm. I called to the doctor, who came back to see about me. I told him that the little boy wanted to know what we were doing there. The doctor shared the gospel with Orlando. Orlando prayed to receive Christ in the midst of utter chaos. Dogs were barking, children were running, the vendors were hawking their wares, but God was there for Orlando. It didn't matter about anything else.

That night we went to the house for the service. I was astonished. The pastor had a living room, a kitchen large enough for only one person, and one bedroom. He had moved the furniture out of the living room and set up folding chairs. His children had been moved in to sleep in the bedroom with the pastor and his wife. He had literally given his house to the Lord. I was outside as we gave the chairs to the people who we hoped would be the founders of this new church. You have seen cows in the country looking through the barn windows. Well, we were standing outside looking into the windows. There was no glass, but shutters that closed. Suddenly I heard my name being called. I went to see what the doctor wanted. He took my hand and led me into the house. There sat Orlando. He had come to church. After the service was over and the pastor made an alter call, Orlando went forward to share his new faith in Jesus Christ. I was walking on air. Look what God had done in the middle of chaos with a doctor who spoke no English and an American who spoke only individual Spanish words and understood almost nothing. Nothing is too big for our God.

THE MACHO MAN

We were in Mexico where I was paired with a national we will name Virginia. Virginia was talking to an older woman in a house when I noticed a young woman outside. I discovered she could understand my feeble attempts at Spanish and my gestures. She would read the Spanish tract for us and we had the people to answer the questions. Several men and women accepted Christ in that house that day.

After we left the house, we talked to a number of people on the street. Several of them accepted Christ. We noticed that one of the young men who had been in the house had followed us, though we didn't know why. We were stopped on the street talking to two young girls when another young man came up to us. Now this was a huge "macho-type" young man who wore his shirt unbuttoned. If I had met him in a dark alley I would have been scared to death. Virginia was witnessing to the young girls when this "macho-man" started talking in Spanish. I told him, "*Un momento, Señor.*"

He would wait a minute then start interrupting again. Since this happened several times, I wasn't sure if he was harassing us or not.

13

Finally he started to leave, so I said, *"Señor, permanece por favor aquí,"* translated 'Sir, please stay here'. He started to leave, but the young man who had been following us grabbed this huge "macho-man" and forced him between himself and me. When Virginia finished witnessing to the girls, I said, "Virginia*, el Señor."*

Virginia began her witnessing to the "macho-man". Meanwhile the young man who had followed us went into another house and brought out three old kitchen chairs and set them in the middle of the dirt street. This was a strange sight – a "macho-man", a young national and a blonde headed woman - sitting in old kitchen chairs in the middle of a dirt street. Virginia went through the questions, but the big man's heart was hard. She would turn to scriptures in the Bible to answer his many questions. When he would start the Prayer of Forgiveness, he would stop before completing it and ask another question. Three times he started and three times he stopped. Now, I had no idea what was being said once they had left the tract. The fourth time the "macho-man" started the prayer, he went straight through it. I wish everyone could have seen his face at that moment. The transformation was incredible. We left him, asking him to share

14

his faith in Christ with his friends. The presence of the Holy Spirit was very strong.

We never leave those who accept Christ behind without follow-up. We take their names and addresses and give them to the pastor of the Mother Church we are working with. The church has teams who do Bible studies with them and take them to church. These new believers build the body of the new mission church we are starting. They are also given a preacher for the new mission church. The new mission church is supported in all ways by the Mother Church. The new mission church must send a monthly report back to Global Missions Fellowship and E- Partnership for one year. This way we know it is a viable church. If they are struggling, we will have a team return and help them.

Through the help of the Lord, we start mission churches that will stand until the Lord returns for His Children.

TIRED, DIRTY AND OVERWHELMED

Another day, another miracle from God. We had been working all day witnessing from door to door and on the streets to anyone who wanted to listen. The doctor had not worked today as he had to be at the hospital, so I was assigned a young woman to work with me. Rosa spoke some English. I was walking toward the pastor's house feeling tired, and knew it was time to go in to eat and then have service. Rosa came to me and said, "There is a family here that I would really like you to talk with. The man has asked us to explain why we have come." He came outside and introduced himself; he also spoke English. Thank you, Lord. I told him I was so very tired, and would he mind if we sat down on the sidewalk to talk. I told him we had come to share our love of Jesus and to start a new Mission Church in their neighborhood. After explaining the plan of salvation, he prayed to receive Jesus as his Savior. He and his two small children went back inside their house and I still sat on the sidewalk. I suddenly thought, "I am so tired, so dirty, so hot, I don't speak the language. I don't know what I am eating and I have never been happier in my life!"

16

LANGUAGE MISUNDERSTANDING

Another service is held in the pastor's home. It was early and not

many people were there. The pastor started talking to me. I

understood him to ask if this was my first trip to Mexico City. I said,

"Si." Everyone clapped and cheered, but the interpreter started saying

loudly, "No, No!" It seems I had just agreed to not return to the

United States, and to live in Mexico and continue working with the

new Mission Church. I quickly explained through the interpreter that I

did not think my husband would be happy with my living in Mexico

City, but I would love to return on another mission trip!

The car is locked up while we held night services.

THE FISH

The leader of the mission organization had repeatedly told us "If you don't speak fluent Spanish, do not attempt to witness in Spanish. Speak in English in short statements that complete the thought, then let the interpreter interpret before you continue." Well, this one American man thought he could speak Spanish well enough to do it himself, after all that is what he had come for – to not let someone else speak for him. He started witnessing to this lady on the street. His interpreter saw a friend nearby and decided to visit since he wasn't needed to interpret. Eventually the interpreter realized there was a problem and asked George what the problem was. George said, "I have repeatedly asked this lady if she believed she was a sinner and she keeps shaking her head no. I just can't convince her that she is a sinner." The interpreter said, "Say to me what you have said to her." George replied, "Do you believe you are a *pescado*?" The interpreter laughed and said, "You just asked her if she believed she was a fish! This is why she keeps shaking her head no. Ask her if she believes she is a '*pecador*'." She eagerly replied, "Oh, *si senor*." Obviously

George didn't witness in Spanish anymore, and the lady accepted the Lord.

INTERPRETER HUMOR

It was our last night and I wanted to give some gifts to the Mexican nationals who had been so kind to me all week. I asked a fourteen year old boy who spoke English to translate for me. I told him I had brought some gifts for the doctor and his wife. I gave the doctor's wife the gift with no problem. Then I told the translator to tell the doctor that my husband used Old Spice cologne and I thought he might enjoy it also. The look on the doctor's face told me that was not what my interpreter said. I grabbed hold of the boy and said, "What did you say?" He was doubling up laughing. I managed in my one word Spanish to get across to the doctor that my husband used this and I thought he might like it also. It seems the boy told the doctor that he stinks and I was giving this to him because he smelled so bad! Oh well, no harm done and teenagers are teenagers no matter what country.

AIRLINE PERSONNEL LAUGH OF THE DAY

In 1987, I called the airlines and asked for the baggage department. This very nice man came on the phone and I asked him if the baggage compartment was pressurized. He said, "Yes it is, but why would you want to know that?" I told him I wanted to put some canned soft drinks in my luggage and I didn't want them exploding. He cracked up laughing and said, "Lady, you can buy cans of soft drinks all over the world. Why would you want to take them in your luggage?" I told him I was a short term missionary and we were not always where we could buy Cokes because of our time and transportation limitations. He replied, "Lady, you just go right ahead and put those Cokes in your luggage and I guarantee they will not explode!"

SPANISH VERSUS SPANISH

On one of our trips I had found a "tende" which is a very, very small stall that sells something. In this case it was on the sidewalk a block from our hotel. I went down every few days and I would say, "*Senor, por favor.*" Then I would hold up three fingers and say, "*Tres* Coca Colas." Then I would use my hands to imitate the opening of a coke and say, "*Nada.*" The man laughed and gave me three unopened Cokes. I would go back next time and he would already have them out for me. The last day, one of our ladies came to me and said, "Alene, haven't you been buying Cokes from that *tende*? Sue speaks fluent Spanish and the man couldn't understand what she wanted." I took Sue down there and the man said, "*Tres* Coca Colas *nada.*" I laughed and said, "No, *uno* Coca Cola," made the opening motion with my hands and said, "*Si.*" He gave Sue the opened Coca Cola and she was astounded. She said, "I can't believe I speak fluent Spanish and you do your one word Spanish with hand motions and he understands you, not me!" She then thanked me and enjoyed her Coke.

Jeannie Tidwell

LETTER FROM ALENE

April 25, 1997

Dear Christian Friends,

I can't believe it has been a year since we moved to Trinity. As you know we firmly believe that God moved us here. We know there is a purpose and we have only to wait on Him to guide us. We have been happy here and have made many new friends.

I'm continuing the missions work in which I was involved in Houston. I had earnestly prayed for God to reveal to me if I was to continue. Without a doubt my prayer was answered in Venezuela.

Every trip is different. This was my 17th mission trip and God made this one so special. We only had 14 Americans to go, but God was faithful and really revealed himself in Venezuela.

Update on the mission trips from Trinity:

DATE	Location	# new mission churches	Received Jesus Christ
8/96	Bogota, Columbia	9	1099
11/96	Lima & Chince, Peru	24	1725
3/97	Valencia, Venezuela	8	425

25

I want to share with you just one experience out of many from these three trips.

We were assigned our national workers and we started out. Ilsa asked us to go to this young woman's house. Ilsa was a great witness but many would not let her witness to them. So Ilsa asked if a lady from the United States would come and talk with them.

We walked through the house and sat in the back yard on old lawn chairs because there was no furniture in the house to sit on. We started witnessing to her and Migdahlia prayed to receive Christ as her Savior. While Ilsa was getting her name and address down for follow-up, I saw a movement behind a huge palm tree. I asked Rolando who the old man was in the back yard. He, in turn, asked Migdahlia. She said he was a crazy old man who had nowhere to live and they permitted him to live in their back yard. Rolando and I walked over there. The old man was sitting on a little child's chair. He was incredibly dirty and so was the area in which he lived. There was a tiny building that was full of his things. He apparently slept on the floor there when the weather was bad. We each took one of his hands, put our arm around him and prayed for him.

26

In the meantime Migdahlia's brother had come to visit her and little did he know that God had a surprise for him! After witnessing to him, he also prayed to receive Christ.

We left, but the next day we went back to do the follow-up Bible study. Migdahlia was in bed sick and the old man was not there. The next day (Wednesday), I was working with the pastor of the mother church. We had just left a home where a man and woman had received Christ. We were supposed to go to the pastor's house for lunch, but I saw we were close to Migdahlia's house. I told him I had to go back there.

He said, "But we must go to lunch."

I told him of the old man, and he said, "Yes, we must go there."

We arrived to find God had provided us time to witness to the old man. Migdahlia was bathing her baby and asked us to wait in the back yard. We went over to the old man and again he did not acknowledge us. I asked the pastor to do the witnessing and not to worry about my part.

He said, "No, Alene, you must do this."

I explained that I didn't speak Spanish and he wouldn't understand my poor attempt.

He said, "Yes, you must read the tract in Spanish."

I started out with "Do you believe in God?"

The old man looked up and said, "*Si.*"

I continued on and the further down the tract I read, the straighter the old man sat, and the clearer his eyes and the stronger his voice. After I finished the tract, I asked him if he would like to pray to receive Christ. He said, "Si."

The pastor asked him his name. It was Juan Moreno. "How old are you, Juan?"

The old man didn't know.

"What year were you born?" asked the pastor.

The old man didn't know.

We gave him a new Testament and went back to do discipleship training with Migdahlia. While the pastor was doing this, I watched the old man. He was still reading the New Testament when we left. The pastor had an appointment to go back to do discipleship training with the old man on the Saturday we flew back to Houston.

Please pray for the nationals. They have the real work to do after we leave. They must do follow-up and disciple all of these people.

It is such a privilege God has given to me to be a little part of His Kingdom's work. It is such a joy to lead people to the saving knowledge of Jesus Christ. I am thankful the Holy spirit always goes before us preparing hearts to receive the Lord Jesus.

Your sister in Christ,

Alene Dalley

Matthew 9: 37-38

Then saith He unto His disciples, the harvest truly is plenteous, but the laborers are few. Pray ye therefore the Lord of the harvest, that He will send forth laborers into His harvest.

THE VOLCANO

As a hurricane moved out in the Atlantic Ocean, it progressively moved toward Nicaragua. The hurricane moved over land and stalled, sitting there for three days. Havoc was wrecked on that small country. Trees were downed, roads were washed out, homes and crops destroyed and people had died.

Through Global Missions Fellowship, Sagemont Church was sending a mission team in to offer aid and Jesus. My husband and I had been members of Sagemont Church for twenty-eight years. Even though we now lived in Trinity, Texas, I went with the team.

We shipped fifty-pound bags of maize, rice and beans. Then we bought cots in Nicaragua. We went out into the countryside where little help would be given. The cities were getting help but the damage was not as great as in the countryside.

The nationals took us by bus into the countryside so we could determine how best we could help. We got out of the bus at one point and were walking over hard-crusted dirt. Tiny bits of wood, almost like toothpicks, lay all over the ground. I asked one of the nationals what they were. He pointed to the dense forest in the distance and said the whole area was once covered with forest like that.

The hurricane had been over the area for three days and had poured heavy rain into two volcanoes located near each other.

One of the volcanoes was active, so the rain had evaporated as soon as it hit the fire inside the volcano. The other volcano was inactive and had gradually filled with water. The force from the weight of the water gradually pushed on the mud sides of the volcano, eventually breaking it down. Thousands of gallons of mud and water were released over a little village. The volcano had burst in the early morning hours while the people were sleeping. The roar woke some of the people in time for them to evacuate their huts. Those who ran in front of the mud slide were overtaken and died. A few villagers who lived on the edge of town ran to the side and survived. We realized we were walking on the graves of hundreds of people. It was a humbling but uncomfortable feeling and we immediately went back to the bus.

The national took us to a church that was actually on the back side of the volcano. At one point, on our way there, the road was washed out, so we had to drive across the lower part of the river. We arrived at the church and talked with the pastor. He introduced us to a woman who lived in the area. She said many people would come for the food, but she would know whose homes had been destroyed and really deserved the aid.

We returned to our hotel to meet and make a game plan for giving out the maize, rice, beans and cots. The hotel was very old but clean and actually interesting. When you entered, there was the check-in desk and a small dining room to the left. Heading straight past the desk through columns was an outdoor veranda. There we found many beautiful, extremely comfortable wooden rocking chairs. I thought, "I wish there was a way to get two of these rocking chairs home to Texas." From the veranda, you would go to your room. The building was two-story built in a square around the veranda and beautiful gardens.

The next day we went back to the church. The people lined up at a side door. They had to get by the lady who knew everyone. After the needy were signed in, they would be sent to a waiting area on the far side of the building while the food was sacked up for them according to how many people were in the family. We were in that area sitting in folding chairs with an empty chair facing each of us. There, we gave the plan of salvation. They already knew this was not required of them to receive rations. Many accepted Jesus as Savior and some did not. All of the food and cots were given out and we could have given out more.

After we finished, the nationals said they wanted to show us something. We walked away from the church a short distance and saw hot lava pools everywhere. The national said the children play there, jumping from stone to stone. The previous day a little girl's foot slipped into a hot pool of lava and she had to be taken to the hospital.

The national then led us across the rocks showing us more and more of the volcano. I wondered what in the world we were doing stepping across hot pools of lava. A couple of people continued on with the national, but most of us returned to the church. The risk was not worth it and we had more work to do.

The next day we went into a different village. There we witnessed to anyone who would listen. I always take used eye-glasses with me. I asked one of the nationals to tell people to come to me if they had seeing problems and might need glasses.

I had just given a woman a pair of eye glasses and asked her to read John 3:16 from a Bible. A man in a suit walked up to me and asked what I was doing. I told him I had brought eyeglasses for those who needed them and could not afford to buy them. He asked me how I knew what prescription they needed. I thought, "Oh boy! This is a government man and I am in trouble!" I explained that I gave them different pairs until they could read the scripture.

He said, "Good! Keep up the good work. I am an ophthalmologist and the government just sent me out to evaluate the damage and needs."

I thought, "Wow, an ophthalmologist just validated the work I have done all over the world with giving out these eyeglasses." By having them read the scripture John 3:16 I was also able to witness to them.

Another day we went to a subdivision to do door-to-door witnessing. We ran into another group of Americans who were upset and crying. We went over to them to see what was wrong and if there was anything we could do to help. They had just gotten word that their pastor in Houston had died. They were trying to decide whether they should go home for the funeral or stay and work. Finally, they decided Pastor Osteen would want them to stay and lead people to the Lord.

When you are on a mission trip you are out of touch with what goes on at home and in the world. One time in another country we received word through the nationals that Premier Gorbachev of Russia had been kidnapped. They told us that they didn't know what was going on and thought it a possibility that the United States was under attack. We had a prayer breakfast that morning beyond compare as we prayed for the Premier and for the United States and all our families and friends. That afternoon we were able to find out more detail, and that there was not an attack on the USA. But while we were going door to door witnessing that day, we didn't know. Everything is in God's control and we just had to have faith.

We went to the airport in Nicaragua and one of our young men asked me how many suitcases I was checking. We could check two, but I only had one, so he asked if he could check a crated rocking chair under my name. He was taking seven unassembled rocking chairs back to the United States. I tried to talk him out of one, but he already had them designated for family and friends. I let him put the package under my name, but I wish I had thought of that!

THE STRAWBERRIES

When we go on mission trips, we are told to avoid drinking the water, do not use the ice, and don't eat anything that isn't cooked or that can't be peeled. Also, if your plate, glass or utensils are wet from washing, be sure to dry them off for a few seconds before using them.

Our church planter took his teenaged daughter and her friend along on a mission trip to Peru. Word got around that the two girls became really sick. Before we left to work, my roommate and I went to their room to pray for them. When I walked into the room, one of the girls said, "Mrs. Dalley, we're sick and can't go out to work." I told them God had not sent them to Peru to stay in bed. Wait and see how God would use it.

At that time we did not know why they were sick. Mike called for a doctor to come. We were on the third floor and there was no elevator. The doctor was crippled, so his nurse who was also his fiancé helped him climb the stairs. After questioning the girls, the doctor discovered they had eaten fresh strawberries. They were not cooked and could not be peeled. They were a "no-no" for eating. He gave them medication, then he turned to Mike and said, "May I sit down? I'm so tired from the stairs." Mike found the doctor a chair.

The doctor said, "I have been looking for someone to tell me about God. Could you tell me about God?" Mike was the church planter leader, so of course he could tell the doctor about God. After Mike talked to the doctor and his nurse, they both accepted Christ as Savior.

I went to see the girls when I returned to the hotel that evening, and they were both excited. They said, "Mrs. Dalley, you were right! You won't believe what happened." They told me about the doctor and nurse and how they had accepted the Lord. The girls admitted they didn't mind being sick since they had witnessed God's purpose in using them to lead two more people to the Lord.

STARVATION

I am not a big eater, so I had not taken any snacks with me except, of course, my Cokes to drink. By the way, at home I would never consider drinking Cokes any other way than ice cold. On mission trips you soon learn if you want a Coke, you will learn to drink it very warm and enjoy it. We went to the mission site the first day of this mission trip and worked all morning. Then we went back to the mission church building as the ladies were bringing our lunch there. They walked in with a five gallon paint bucket with yellow, red, blue and green paint around the top and sides. Inside the bucket was a pasta mixture. I thought, "How am I going to handle this, as you must never insult anyone, and to not eat their food would be an insult." I told the lady that ladled the soup into our bowls, "*Un poco, me esposo* would not like for me to gain weight." Every day after that, I got a couple of tablespoons of the lunch and no dinner. I was about to starve. I told my roommate about it and the only thing she had was a bag of salted sunflower seeds. She said that after we took our showers, we would share them. She took her shower then I took mine. She said, "I will eat my half while you shower." When I went into the room after my shower, she looked a little shocked and said, "I got

carried away. I was so hungry that I ate the whole bag." We laughed

and we both learned a lesson. Take food.

FOOD FIT FOR A KING (OR QUEEN)

On another trip to Mexico City, my teammate and I were way out of the city and into the mountains. We had to walk, and then ride a bus, then walk, then take a taxi and finally another bus. We met our national teammates and started working. At lunch, the interpreter took the two of us to a lady's house for lunch. The interpreter said we would be eating there every day for lunch and dinner. Maria, our hostess, served us a very large bowl of green soup. I was skeptical, but I always prayed for God to help me eat whatever was put before me and not get sick nor offend my hostess. I tasted the green soup expecting it to be split pea. It was not split pea, but was the best soup I had ever tasted in my life. I ate the whole bowl thinking that was all the lunch. Maria took our bowls and brought us a plate with a huge piece of roast with potatoes and vegetables. I was already full, but I ate anyway. Then she brought our dessert – the best flan I had ever eaten.

We told her we could not eat as much as she served. She laughed at us gringos and said that the amount she had cooked for three adults was less than she would have cooked for herself, her husband and their ten year old son. We told her that she was feeding us so well at lunch that we would prefer to get back to the hotel right after church every night rather than wait for dinner to be cooked and be so late getting to bed. She agreed that would be just fine. So after church that evening, she brought us chocolate banana milkshakes. She had brought a blender and all of the ingredients from home and fixed it for us every night. Wonderful!

We got back to the hotel that night and the church planter, Mike, came running up to me and hugged me. He said, "Where have you been?"

"I have been to the mission site and the church service. Why are you asking?"

He said, "I always visit each mission site to be sure everything is okay. I started out to your site and couldn't find anyone who had ever heard of that name. I thought I had lost my whole team!"

I called the interpreter over and had him give Mike directions. The next evening here was Mike. After the service, Maria brought him a milkshake along with ours. He asked if we got this kind of treatment every day. We laughed and told him, "Of course!" Mike said, "I don't have to worry any more about this team."

GOD'S LANGUAGE

One night we were at a home having a service when a family singing group came in. They said they had heard we were there and wondered if they might share their music for the service. They were wonderful. They could really sing and loved to sing praises to the Lord. A young man came to stand by me and said, "I will interpret for you." I suddenly realized I understood everything they sang. I told him I could understand it, so he asked how that was possible since I didn't speak Spanish. The only thing I could say was that it was a gift from the Lord.

GOD'S LOVING CARE

I had a mission trip scheduled when I received a call from my aunt. She had had heart bypass surgery only a couple of months before and now my cousin had had a heart attack and stroke. She had just come out of a coma and the family needed someone to help sit with her. I left the next day to help them and sat at the hospital from 8:00 A.M. until 10:00 P.M. for ten days. I was exhausted. My mother also lived in Oklahoma, so I drove to her house to spend the night with her on my way back home to Houston. I called my husband and said, "I have an upper respiratory infection and I need some antibiotics." I knew I would not get home in time to get the antibiotics and prepare adequately for my mission trip. My husband was able to get the antibiotics, so I flew out on my mission trip. I told the Church Planter's assistant, a wonderful lady, that I was sick and wasn't sure I could make it all day. I asked if she could put me as close to the hotel as possible in case I couldn't make the afternoon. She was my teammate, and the first day we worked all morning. We went to this wonderful family's home for lunch.

After lunch we thought we were going back out to work, but the lady of the house told us to come with her, where she showed us a bedroom with two beds. "It is so hot here that we do not go back out until 3:00. You may have a rest until then." Thank you Lord. God knew I could not have made the day without that rest. Never before had I ever had a place to rest before going back out to work the afternoon. God never sends you out without equipping you with whatever you need.

MOUNTAINS MADE BY GOD

A request had come to the missions organization for us to send a team into a town in the Sierra Madre Mountains. A preacher there knew of the work this organization was doing, and since the staff was acquainted with him, it was not necessary to follow the usual pattern. The normal procedure is to send a church planter in to check everything out and make all the arrangements. Next, a team of pastors go in to train the leaders who will be pastoring the new mission churches. They make sure the theology is the same. The lay people similar to me go in next to witness and help build the body of the church. Since normal procedure was not followed, it was everyone's first time into this area. A large tour bus was sent to pick us up, and off we went. Soon we were on a narrow road. I was seated by a window, and when I looked down, all I could see were trees below. On the other side, the bus was scraping the side of the mountain. It was an adventure and we all enjoyed the excitement…that is, until the bus driver decided to pass an eighteen wheeler on a curve. We decided this might be a little more excitement than we needed. Many people were led to the Lord because we were willing to take that bus ride. Our church planter said no other team would go in until they had

a runway and could fly in.

"THE VISION"

This story was written by one of the 25 missionaries. I do not know whom to give the credit.

In the beginning there were 25 and each in their own time and in their own place were born and their names were: Dave, Larry, Lou, Steve, David, Bob D., Bob G., John Wi., Charlie, Sonny, Eric, Charles Mc., Brandy, Alene, Bob H., Maria, Bobbie, Renee, Phil, Jeremy, Alberto, Stephanie, John We., Charlie W., and Rosie.

None of them were righteous, not even one. There was not one of them who understood. There was not one of them who sought God. All of them turned away. They together became worthless. There was not one of them who did good, not even one. (Romans 3: 10-13)

They tried to live life on their own strength, in their own way and they became tired. And Jesus came to each one of them in their own time and said to them, "Come to me, all you who are weary and burdened, and I will give you rest. Take my yoke upon you and learn from me for I am gentle and humble in heart, and you will find rest for your souls. For my yoke is easy and my burden is light." (Matthew 11: 28-30)

So each one in his own time and in his own way said "yes" to Jesus and was given joy and life. In the fullness of time they became aware of those around them who did not know Jesus. They heard their Lord say, "The harvest is plentiful, but the workers are few. Ask the Lord of the harvest, therefore, to send out workers into the harvest field." (Matthew 9:37)

So each one of them in their own time and in their own way began to pray for workers but the Lord said to each of them, "The Spirit of the Sovereign Lord is on you because the Lord has anointed you to preach good news to the poor. He is sending you to bind up the brokenhearted, to proclaim freedom for the captives and release from darkness for the prisoners, to proclaim the year of the Lord's favor." (Isaiah 61: 1-2)

Each of them responded to the Lord and went to San Marcos, Nicaragua, and they became the 25. And I saw the 25 preach the good news to people and bind up their broken hearts and heal their illnesses. I saw them give a kind word and a smile. I saw them give them an umbrella and clothes and blankets. I saw them visit the sick, and give them something to eat and drink. I saw them invite them in and pray for them.

So it came to pass that many Nicaraguans came to know the Lord.

After this, I saw the Lord in heavenly glory seated on His throne. All the nations were gathered before Him, the 25 were there, and the Nicaraguans were there. He separated the people one from another as a shepherd separates the sheep from the goats. He put the 25 and many Nicaraguans with the sheep on His right and the goats on His left.

Then the King said to those on His right, "Come you who are blessed by my Father. Take your inheritance, the kingdom prepared for you since the creation of the world. For I was hungry and you gave me something to eat. I was thirsty and you gave me something to drink. I was a stranger and you invited me in. I needed clothes and blankets and you clothed me. I was sick and you looked after me. I was in prison and you came to visit me."

The 25 will say, "Lord when did we see you hungry and feed you or see you thirsty and give you something to drink? When did we see you a stranger and invite you in, or see you needing clothing and blankets and clothe you? When did we see you sick or in prison and go visit you?"

The King will reply, "I tell you the truth. Whatever you did for one of the least of these brothers of mine, the Nicaraguans, the low ones, you did for me." (Matthew 25: 31-40)

Then the Lord will say to the 25, "Well done my good and faithful servants! You have been faithful with a few things. I will put you in charge of many things. Come and share your Master's happiness!" (Matthew 25:21)

After this I looked and there before me was a great multitude that no one could count. From every nation, tribe, people and language, and the 25 were there, and the Nicaraguans, standing before the throne and in front of the Lamb. They were wearing white robes and were holding palm branches in their hands. They cried out in a loud voice, "Salvation belongs to our God who sits on the throne and to the Lamb!" (Revelations 7: 9-10)

Then I saw many of the Nicaraguans go to the 25 and say,

"Thank you for giving to the Lord.

I am a life that was changed.

53

Thank you for giving to the Lord.

I am so glad you gave!"

Amen and Amen!

MIRACLE AFTER MIRACLE AFTER MIRACLE

It was the first day in the neighborhood and we met our nationals. We were waiting for other nationals to come. I was sitting there and noticed a girl glaring at me. Finally she said, "May I ask you a question?"

"Of course," I replied.

"You are wearing a cross. What does it mean to you?" she asked.

I told her it represented the cross my Savior died on. I asked her what it meant to her. She said that she thought it meant you love Catholics. Well, of course I do. I explained to her that there is a difference between my cross and the Catholic cross. The Catholic cross shows Jesus is still on the cross. She would have nothing to do with me. I thought this was the strangest thing I have ever had to happen. Mike, our church planter, came out that night and I told him the problem. He explained to her about the cross and told her I had put it inside my blouse so as not to offend her. We worked all week, and toward the end of the week, she began working with me. I couldn't understand a Christian who had an objection to wearing the cross. That night she came to me and apologized. She said she had watched me all week and now she understood. She asked me for a favor. I had learned that you never promise anything on a mission trip because something may happen, and you could not keep that promise. I asked her what favor, and she replied, "I have a sister in California and she is not a believer. Would you go to her house and tell them about Jesus?" I tried to explain that it was about as far from my home to California as it was from my home to her home. But I would try to find someone to go to her sister. She gave me her sister's name and address.

After we flew home, the next day I prayed for help from God to complete this mission. I called the operator and told her I wanted to speak to any Baptist Church in this particular town.

"Any Baptist Church?"

"Yes, any Baptist Church."

The operator gave me the name of a church and a phone number. I called and explained to the secretary I was calling from Texas, and asked for the pastor's name. She wanted to know why I had called the church if I didn't even know who I was calling. I told her I had been on a mission trip and it was a long story. She told me to call back at 3:00 P.M. and she would have the pastor waiting for my call. When I called back at 3:00, the pastor answered the phone. I explained what had happened on the mission trip. I told him I had no idea where this address was, but I needed someone to go to this home and witness to these people. The pastor laughed and said, "This address is three blocks from this church. I have the perfect person to go witness to them." Then he asked me which church I attended. I explained that I went through a missions organization, not my church, but told him the name of my church – Sagemont Baptist Church. He immediately said, "John Morgan." The two had gone to seminary together some twenty years before. The pastor asked me if I would go to my pastor and tell him that he was trying to build a new sanctuary in California and had run out of money. My pastor John Morgan just happened to be going all over the United States teaching churches how to be debt free. When I told John the story, he immediately called the California church and flew out there to help with the new sanctuary.

Only God could have orchestrated all of that. I was so astounded how it all came together. Then I thought, "What is wrong with me?" Why should I be surprised what God can do? He created the Heavens and the Earth as well as you and me. Why would God have any problem orchestrating my flying to Mexico City, meeting a girl who questioned me and asked me to talk with her sister even though I am from Texas and her sister was in California, my calling the operator and getting the church nearest her sister and connecting with a pastor who was having financial problems and knew my pastor from seminary twenty years before. My pastor was the answer to their problems. Thank you Lord for Your using your children to be a part of Your Kingdom's Work.

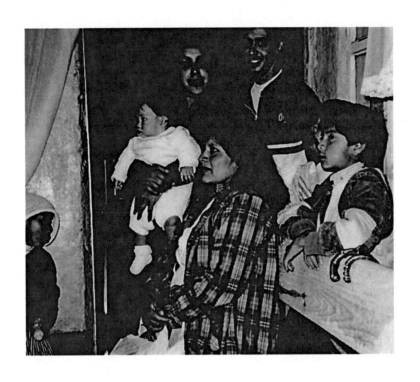

A DRESS FOR LENA

After having worked in this area several days and seeing this woman who was obviously physically afflicted, one of the nationals asked me to guess her age. I said, "Oh no, I am not playing that game!" They kept on asking me, including Lena. I finally guessed her age and guessed her about twenty years older than she actually was. I was heartsick and would not have offended her for any reason. That was our last day and we would be flying out the next day. Lena had told me earlier how much she liked my dress. Well, I had just bought it there in her city so that I would have another mission dress. When the interpreter returned us to our hotel, I asked him to wait in the lobby and I would be right back. I went upstairs, changed clothes, wrapped the dress I had been wearing and went back down to the lobby. I gave him the package and told him it was a gift for Lena. I could just imagine Lena opening up that package and seeing that new dress and all of her friends being so envious. I hope that her friends would be nicer to her and would not ridicule Lena as they had in the past.

PERSECUTED

I was assigned to Mission Filadelphia. My national was Lettie. Lettie was just as sweet as she could be, but her face was disfigured. I never asked her what caused it. I just took Lettie as she was – a good Christian who loved the Lord and wanted to serve Him. The first day we went out to witness, Lettie said, "I would like to take you on the bus so you will see more." I thought that was strange, as we needed to witness close to the mission site, but I went along with her. Another day Lettie wanted to take me to this special place to witness. This went on all week with many accepting Christ.

Then one day Lettie became very nervous and started crying. I asked her what was wrong. Lettie said, "That lady was a friend of mine and she will tell my husband what I am doing." I asked her if her husband did not want her to witness for Christ. Lettie just let it all out and told me the reason her face was disfigured. Her husband beats her. Once before, he caught her with their two small children at a church service, and he had dragged her and the two boys out by force. This was the reason she had steered me to places all week where she would not meet anyone she knew. We went to the pastor and talked

61

with him since Lettie was afraid to go home. The pastor went to Lettie's house and tried to talk to her husband. He was not receptive, but the pastor let him know there had better not be any more beating of Lettie or the children else he would find himself in much trouble. All of us prayed for Lettie and her family when we left her in the care of her pastor.

DEMON POSSESSED

If you had asked me what I believed about demon possession in the 20th century, I would have had to think about it. I no longer have to think about it. I have seen it firsthand. I had read about it in the Bible, but we tend to think that some of those things couldn't happen now. Satan is as active now as he was in the biblical days.

Mark and I were assigned this beautiful young girl as our national. The only problem was she didn't speak any English and we didn't have enough translators. Since Mark and I both could manage a few words, we agreed to let the others have the translators.

Each day we would walk about a mile from the mission site to the pastor's house to eat lunch. Each day we left to go back to the mission site and witness to people in the streets and knock on doors. People were accepting Jesus as Savior and each night we had a service. One day was different. For some reason, the three of us could not get our act together to get ready and leave at the same time. Finally, everyone else had gone. All the teams were out witnessing except ours, plus the pastor and his wife. We were almost an hour and a half late leaving. We were not supposed to witness in the area of the pastor's house, only in the mission area. As we left, I handed out a small booklet of Bible verses in Spanish to this young man in the street and walked on by. I looked around and Esmeralda and Mark had stopped to talk with him, so I went back. Esmeralda gave the plan of salvation and gave the young man paper and pencil. When he started to fill the paper out saying he had accepted Christ as his Savior, he started violently swinging his arm. He could not put the pencil on the paper. Finally, it was accomplished and we were bowing our heads to pray for his affliction. Mark prayed that God would remove from him whatever was causing his problem. Suddenly, Esmeralda let out a blood-curdling scream and ran to the pastor's home and beat on the door. She knocked the pastor back against the wall when he opened the door. Esmeralda ran into the kitchen where the pastor's wife was working. The pastor asked me what had happened. I opened my Spanish dictionary and showed him the word "demonic." He read the Spanish definition and told us to wait there. The pastor went into the kitchen and talked with Esmeralda. He came back and asked for the paper. He told us that we would not follow up on this one. He would take deacons from his church to the man's home that afternoon. The

64

three of us left to return to the mission site, but Esmeralda was in no shape to witness. She would just wander off as if in a daze. Finally, we gave up and went back to the mission site. Mark and I only had a new testament, but Esmeralda kept asking for a Bible. Another team came by and loaned us a Bible. Esmeralda grabbed it and turned to Psalms 91.

> *I will say of the Lord, he is my refuge and my fortress:*
>
> *my God; in him will I trust. Surely He shall deliver*
>
> *thee from the snare of the fowler, and from the noisome*
>
> *pestilence. He shall cover thee with his feathers, and*
>
> *under his wings shalt thou trust: his truth shall be thy*
>
> *shield and buckler. Thou shalt not be afraid for the*
>
> *terror by night; nor the arrow that flieth by day.*

Esmeralda was telling us God had protected us from the evil one. We still didn't understand everything that had happened. That night a young man showed up at the evening service. He came to me and said, "I was told that an interpreter was needed here tonight." I knew God had sent him to us. I took him to Mark and Esmeralda, and I told the young man what had happened that day. We asked him to ask

Esmeralda what had happened and why she had screamed and run away. After he had talked to her in Spanish, he turned to us and said, "When Mark prayed that God would remove whatever was causing the young man's affliction, a demon manifested itself. Since Esmeralda was in front of him and looking at him while you both had your heads bowed, Esmeralda saw the demon.

Mark 3:14-15:

And He appointed twelve, that they might be with

Him and that He might send them out to preach, and

to have authority to cast out the demons.

Mark 5: 2:

And when He had come out of the boat, immediately a

man from the tombs with an unclean spirit met Him

Mark 5: 7-14

...And crying out with a loud voice, he said, "What

do I have to do with You, Jesus, Son of the Most

High God? I implore You by God, do not torment

me!" For He had been saying to him, "Come out of

the man, you unclean spirit!" And he began to

entreat Him earnestly not to send them out of the

country. Now there was a big herd of swine feeding

there on the mountainside. And they entreated Him,

saying, "Send us into the swine so that we may enter

them." And coming out, the unclean spirits entered

the swine; and the herd rushed down the steep bank

into the sea, about two thousand of them; and they

were drowned in the sea.

If you should ever come upon demon possession, do not attempt to remove them unless you have been trained. Go immediately and get help.

TEENAGE SOCCER

Mark, Esmeralda and I were returning from witnessing when it was time for the service. We passed an open field where many teenage boys were playing soccer. I did not want to interrupt them since they may not have appreciated that and would reject what we had to offer. I went up to a huge rock and laid down some booklets containing Spanish Bible verses and just motioned to the boys that I had put something there. As we left, we turned around to watch, and saw about half the boys had left the soccer game and were reading the booklets. We didn't know if anything would come of it, but God's word never comes back void. Later that week some of the boys came to service and accepted the Lord as their personal Savior. It is amazing how easy it sometimes is to witness and how hard we try to make it.

4
Thy word have I hid in mine heart, that I might not sin against thee.
—Ps. 119:11

Every word of God is pure: he is a shield unto them that put their trust in him. —Prov. 30:5

Thy word is truth. —Jn. 17:17

5
Study to shew thyself approved unto God . . .
—2 Tim. 2:15

. . . If ye continue in my word, then are ye my disciples indeed. —Jn. 8:31

. . . every house is builded by some man; but he that

I HAVE BEEN WAITING FOR YOU

Another day, Mark, Esmeralda and I were on our way to service when we saw an old man standing on the corner. I handed him the booklet of verses, and he told Esmeralda in Spanish for us to wait. We did not know what we were waiting for. He left, and returned with a Bible. It had belonged to his father. The old man said, "I have been waiting for someone to come tell me what this book says, for I do not know how to read." Esmeralda told him about the Bible and gave him the plan of Salvation. He readily accepted Christ as His Savior. We went on to the service. The next night, the old man came to the service. When it was time for the invitation, he went forward and told the congregation how he had been standing on the corner waiting for someone to tell him about Jesus, and how he had accepted Jesus into his heart.

LEAVING OUR HEARTS IN VENEZUELA

When we left for the airport to return home, a few of the nationals went with us. What we did not know was that many more nationals had already arrived at the airport just before we did. Since the nationals could not go with us to the airplane, they had climbed upon the roof of the two story airport terminal building. Airplane passengers had to walk out of the tarmac and climb metal stairs to get to the airplane. As we were climbing the stairs, we suddenly heard this loud singing of Christian hymns. We turned to see where it was coming from, and saw there on the roof all of our new friends waving goodbye to us and singing. I don't believe any of us were dry-eyed at that point. It touched us to see that it meant so much to them for us to come work alongside them and tell their countrymen about the Lord Jesus Christ that they would come and serenade our farewell with Christian music.

LETTER FROM A PASTOR

Dear Sister Alene,

May the Lord Jesus Christ be with you and your family.

I want to express you our deep gratitude for the blessings we had during the few days you and James spent in our church. All the people were greatly blessed during the missionary time you was in our church.

Specially, I am very happy to report you about that young man we talked to in Timothy's home. You remember him, who said to you, "I don't believe in God." I sent him the gift you dedicated and also wrote a letter telling him you put his name in your Bible to pray for his soul. Now see what happened: He came to church the following Sunday, with his child and attended my S.S. class, but he

had to leave because child. Next time, on

June 3, he came to see the movie "Jesus",

being very impress with it. On Sunday 7,

he came to church and called me to say,

"I believe in God, I accepted Jesus as

Savior and tell me what I have to do." I

explained him the new life in Christ.

After the preaching, he raised his hand

and stand up during the invitation.

Before this, he asked me your address.

But he had to work now. I instructed him

how to follow Jesus while he was out of

home and Church. Please write him soon

as possible.

This wonderful pastor who wrote me this letter is now at home with

the Lord. While on this earth he suffered much persecution including

being imprisoned for being a true Christian and living his life

faithfully. He did not bend to the demands made on him.

77

KEEPING A LOW PROFILE (HA)

We had been instructed to keep a very low profile in this country. The very first day the nationals were to pick up my team, they came in an old rattletrap car. They killed the engine, met us, and divided us into the different cars. We got into our car and it wouldn't start. Finally, they said for everyone to get out and push the car. Here we Americans were, pushing an old car down the main street of the town. The car finally started and we each hopped in while cracking up laughing. So much for keeping a low profile! Everyone in the country probably knew we were there now.

LAUGHTER IS THE BEST MEDICINE

When we went into the Amazon Jungle the first time, I was surprised to see four young children. There were two boys and two girls, ages 10 and 11. One of the boys belonged to the church planter, and the other was the son of our nurse. Both of the boys stayed with our leader. One of the ladies brought her daughter, and one of the men also brought his daughter. The two little girls and the Mother were assigned as my roommates.

When we first planned to go into the jungle to a particular village, we thought it would be an "air mattress and tent" trip. The people were so grateful we were coming that they had built little cabins for us. The cabins were one room screened-in, and a so-called bathroom.

One night after having worked several days, we were so tired we got silly. The mother Janie and I started laughing at things that had happened on the trip. Her little girl asked why we were laughing, but we just laughed harder. The little girl finally said, "Stop laughing! You are not acting like my Mother." This really set us off.

Finally the little girl said, "Mother, you are scaring me."

Janie and I were out of control. We tried to quit so we wouldn't scare the girls. We also knew it was way past bedtime. With only the screens for walls, we knew we were probably keeping everyone awake. So the four of us went to our screen and raised our voices toward the cabin next to us. We asked them to please be quiet. They were keeping us awake! This cabin was occupied by the church planter's Mother-in-law, the nurse and two other ladies. They really gave us a hard time with teasing the next day. We all knew it was good fun.

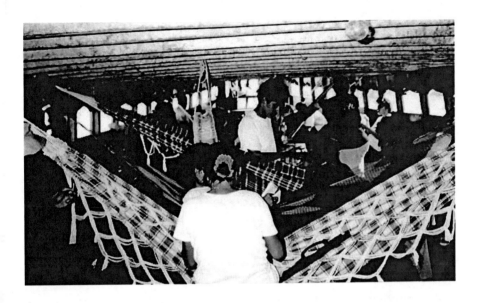

SICK IN THE AMAZON JUNGLE

We had moved from Houston to a small town in East Texas, Trinity, on Lake Livingston. We were in a new church with only a few hundred members, unlike the 16,000 member congregation we left. I was the only one going on mission trips out of this little church. Then we hired a new choir director. I told him about my work and that I was going to the Amazon Jungle.

One night we were having a Sunday School Christmas party and a lady told him, "If you will go to the Amazon with Alene, I will pay for your entire trip." He was shocked and admitted that he had the desire to go. Two months later David Mungle and I were on our way to Peru.

The American missionaries who lived in Iquitos met us at the airport and took us to their home. The whole team stayed there for the night. The next day we had to take two boats far down the Amazon River.

We had worked all week and the morning we were to leave the jungle, one of the young men came to me and said, "David is very sick." We went to his cabin and found him with a high fever and

82

vomiting. Two of the men all but carried him to the boat while others put his luggage, including a guitar, into the boat.

The nurse was in the other boat. She called to me, telling me to take off his shirt and rub him down with hand sanitizer, which contained alcohol. I thought, "Yeah, right, I'm going to start undressing my choir director! I don't care if I am old enough to be his mother, I'm not sure I want to do this!"

David was lying on the board seat opposite me. I went over to his side and could feel the heat radiating from his body. David had on a tee shirt, shorts, socks and tennis shoes. I took off his shoes and socks and rubbed his feet and legs with my hand sanitizer. Then I took a cloth and wet it with bottled water and wiped his face. I poured some of the bottled water on his shirt. It was a three and a half hour boat trip to Iquitos. The guys took David's luggage, but I had to take mine, put his guitar around my neck and my arm around his waist. We had to climb two flights of steep concrete steps to get from the boat to street level. The bus was waiting for us. David was feeling sick at his stomach, so someone gave him an over-the counter tablet. I told David that it wasn't a good idea for him to take it. We used those tablets quite often on mission trips, and couldn't do without them, but this was not the time for David to take one. As soon as the bus stopped at the missionary's house, David was the first one out of the bus, and he threw up the tablet.

Since David was the only one sick, the missionaries gave him the bedroom adjoining a bath. This was to isolate him from the others.

There was another missionary couple in Iquitos, so they called the wife to come check on David. She saw him, went to the hospital pharmacy and requested a little list of items. She didn't need a prescription because they knew her. She only needed the money to pay for the medicines.

The missionary wife returned to the house and started giving David medication plus an electrolyte drink. David was so sick he couldn't even drink. We would have to put the straw in his mouth and coax him.

Later one of the men, the nurse's boy, a little girl, and one of the ladies came down sick. The nurse came to me and said, "Alene, you're going to have to take over all of David's care. My son is sick and I have to take care of him."

I stayed with David, giving him pills and making him drink fluids until 2:00 in the morning, when his fever finally broke. I went to my bed to sleep until 6:00 a.m. when we all got up to make the airline connections.

While all these people were getting sick, our church planter got out his insurance papers. He said, "Alene, our insurance will pay for all these sick people's families to stay until they get well and can catch a later flight. It won't pay for you because you are not any relation to David."

I replied, "I don't care, if you think I'm going back to my church without David, you are mistaken! They would tar and feather me if I came home and left him this sick in Peru."

I was really concerned about David. No one was as sick as he. I just didn't know whether he would recover. But the next morning, David walked into the common area where most of the team had been sleeping in sleeping bags on the floor. We couldn't believe our eyes! Many prayers had been said for David. God took care of all the sick ones. Every one of us made that first flight home.

My husband Mac picked David and me up at the airport in Houston. David started telling Mac about the trip and I started laughing. David had missed a lot by being sick. His perspective was also off. I kept correcting the stories he was telling. David and I have a special bond because of what we went through together.

The missionaries from Peru came to visit my home in Trinity. I invited David and Jackie Mungle to join us all for dinner. I introduced the nurse to Jackie as the lady who literally saved David's life. Jackie gave her a big hug and thanked her. Jackie shared with me later how much it meant to her to meet the missionaries. It is difficult for the spouses to understand what we have been through because life goes on at home.

We later discovered that the people who had been so sick had drunk some water other than bottled water. We took several five-gallon jugs of water, but where we filled our individual bottles in the kitchen, one of the nationals had given them well water instead of the bottled. It was unintentional, because they just didn't understand that we could not drink their water.

All is well that ends well, and I have been back into the Amazon Jungle since this incident..

THE ANACONDA

The entire time we were in the Amazon walking the path from where we were staying to the village and gathering center we never saw a snake. But one day Jewel came to me and said they would be splitting the team. They asked if I would be willing to go by boat to a village further up the Amazon. Half the team remained and the other half left for the village up the Amazon.

As we went by boat, we pulled into a little village along the way and were going to invite the villagers to come to the destination village where we would be showing the Jesus film. The American leader asked me to stay by the village leader's house where a crowd of curious children were gathering. He wanted me to do an impromptu program for the children. We did several things for those children, including a demonstration of the Evangecube. I had noticed a large gathering of adults inside the leader's house. The house was built on stilts and had no walls. I had the children turn around so I could face not only the children but also the adults. As I went through the presentation, I saw one man truly affected. I asked the national to request from the lady of the house permission to go up the steps to her home.   The national quickly said, "No, you cannot do that." I said, "Please, just ask her." To his surprise she said, "Yes." The national and I climbed the stairs, and to my surprise, the people separated. One group came to the middle of the room lined up as if in a meeting. Again, I demonstrated the Evangecube. Those who lined up prayed to receive Christ. The others around the outside of the room did not.

David said I didn't walk down those steps. He said I was so excited and high on the Lord he didn't think my feet ever touched them. One of the people who accepted the Lord had on very outstanding clothing with bright orange and green colors. Therefore, when we got to the destination village I was able to recognize him. He came up to me to thank me for coming. He had come to see the Jesus film.

Three of us ladies were walking the path from hut to hut telling people about the Jesus film and inviting them to come to the open building which was used for a school. We came upon one hut where two children were outside playing with their pets, two-toed sloths.

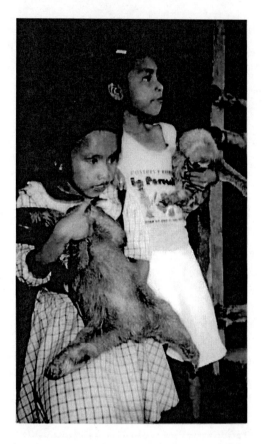

Their Dad was also tending his pet – a huge black snake. I didn't get anywhere near the snake but I petted the sloths. My husband had asked me how I could go into the Amazon when he knows I am so absolutely terrified of snakes. I told him God wants me to go into the Amazon, so he will take care of the Anacondas.

That night we showed the Jesus film to a packed house. The guys had set up a generator. After the film was over, we all climbed into the boat while some of the men were supposed to take down the generator. It seems no one was designated for the job, and everyone except our boat driver and David was at the boat. Suddenly we heard someone screaming. David was running toward our boat while screaming for help. Instead of waiting for the Americans to remove the generator, our boat driver who knew nothing about electricity had tried to take it down alone and received a hefty shock. The Americans ran to help him. He was laid out unconscious with burns on one hand. We had no medical personnel and we feared he was dead. In a few minutes, though, he sat up and the guys helped him stand. The Americans took down the generator and helped the driver back to the boat. One of the Americans offered to drive the boat, but the injured man wouldn't hear of it. We realized he was really the only person who knew how to get us back to our village where we were staying.

It was around midnight by the time we were traveling down the river. The darkness of the Amazon helped reveal a magnificent sky full of stars twinkling like diamonds. One of our people started singing "How Great Thou Art" and we all joined in. We kept singing various Christian songs and felt close to God. What an experience!

The Americans in our home village were all waiting for us in the area where we ate our meals. They were concerned because we were so late. We told them all of what had happened. They told us of some excitement in their village. On the path we walked every day, it seems a little girl had been bitten by an anaconda. The anaconda is not a poisonous snake, and this was a small one, not even large enough to wrap around the little girl. Fortunately our nurse was able to treat the little girl.

Some of the nationals took our "electrocuted" boat driver into Iquitos the next morning to have his burned hand tended. He was fine, also.

EXPERIENCES

We had been in this country several days and had a wide range of experiences. One day I was given this green coconut milk to drink. It was awful to me, but you cannot refuse and risk offending your host. We were shown the view from the window of our hotel and saw these beautiful new hotels that boasted hot water and electricity. We didn't have the hot water and had sporadic blackouts. Another humbling experience was when we were given a tour of the top of our hotel where the hotel laundry was done by hand by poor women. It really made me appreciate what I have back home. But one night at church, a man got up to sing. He had a guitar, raised his eyes to the heavens and sang like an angel. He never once looked at the worshippers. He had eyes and voice only for God. He was an ex drug addict and had turned his life around after he accepted Jesus as Savior.

After church services, another man came to me. He had worked with a team all week, and wanted to witness to me about his belief in God and in receiving Jesus Christ. He had been a high school teacher, but when he accepted the Lord Jesus, he was fired from his job and blacklisted so that he could not get another job. He was homeless, and

93

only by the grace of other Christians did he have a place to stay and food to eat. I wondered how many of us Christians could stand the burdens and persecutions that Christians in other countries live under all the time, yet they still praise the one true God and His son Jesus Christ.

A MAN AFTER GOD'S OWN HEART

I had been assigned to a specific church that had just been started. It would not be planting a new mission, but helping a church to get established with new members. The preacher was friends with a young couple from another denomination. Both denominations had the same basic beliefs. Each believes that God created the Earth in six days, that God created Adam and Eve and everything on the Earth, everything in the seas and in the air. Each believes in God the Father, the Son and the Holy Spirit. Both agree that Jesus was the Son of God, born of a virgin, and that He died on the cross so that all who believe and accept Jesus as Savior might be saved.

I was assigned to work with a young couple, our nationals. Another young man was assigned as my translator. I discovered right away that we had a problem with the translator. I couldn't decide if he wasn't saved or was a brand new Christian. It was not for me to judge, though, so I told him, "Whether you agree with me or not, you are a translator. Translate exactly what I say."

A local had invited us to her home, but when we arrived she was not there. Her Mother was there, but she was of the occult and would

95

not let us in the house. The next door neighbor was watching and invited us to her home. She also asked ten of her neighbors to join us.

I went through our witnessing brochure and many people accepted Christ as Savior. Then I led the people through the first of our Bible studies. All of this was done through the translator. Before we left, I had the translator ask our national what he thought about our witnessing program.

He answered, "It is very long."

I explained, "We completed at one meeting what we normally do in two. Usually the first day we witness, and the next day we go back to those who accepted Christ and do the Bible study."

Since the national had never seen our materials, I wanted him to understand the overall picture. His eyes lit up and he smiled. I didn't know what he was thinking, but you could tell he was running it all through his mind.

We went to lunch at a lady's house. She would provide our lunch all week. Suddenly, I realized we were through eating, ready to leave and our national was not there. We waited and waited until he showed up. He told the translator that we should follow him. We had no idea why. After walking about twenty minutes, we came to a house. The national entered and we followed. There sat twelve men waiting for us.

The national read the first question on our literature and then opened his Bible to the scripture we had noted. He read the scripture from the Bible, then asked each individual for an answer to that first question. He did our entire witnessing program that way. When he finished, all twelve men prayed to receive Christ as their Savior.

I was overwhelmed and elated with this young man's love for God and for his approach in leading his fellow countrymen to the Lord. We left the home to go to dinner followed by our nightly service, then to the hotel for the night.

The next morning our national met us at the church. He took us to a street corner and asked us to stay. We waited thirty minutes before he returned. He took us to another house, and when we entered, there sat a room full of men and women. Again, he went through the presentation followed by reading the scripture from the Bible. Many in that room accepted the Lord.

We left for lunch, but after our meal, the same thing happened again. Another home, more people!

Wednesday morning at our Prayer Breakfast with the entire team, Mike said, "Alene, I have not heard a report from you. What are you doing?"

I said, "Mike, I'm not doing a thing."

"What do you mean you are not doing a thing?!"

I explained what had been happening. He was speechless. He told the rest of the team to see if they had nationals who would work in groups instead of door to door. It seemed to be a waste of time doing our witnessing through interpreters.

That one week our young man personally led three hundred seventy-two people to know Christ as Savior.

A month after we had returned to the USA, I received a letter from the young national's wife. Of course I had to find someone who could translate it for me. She wanted me to know that God had called her husband to preach and he was already enrolled in seminary.

Isn't it wonderful how God puts us all together to work for the good for those who love the Lord.

A SPECIAL GIFT TO ME FROM GOD

We went to the church we would be working through and there I was assigned my national – a lovely young woman named Janet. Janet would be my interpreter. We were told that we could only go to a Christian home to witness. I was taken to a Christian home where we just visited and invited them to church. A lady in her seventies approached me and said she would be unable to come to church that evening because she had no one to stay with her mother who was ninety-one years old. I said, "I understand. Where do you live?"

She said, "Just across the street." I asked if we could go to her house and pray for her mother. She agreed. We walked across the street and into her home. I knelt by her mother's chair and prayed for her. The elderly mother said it was the first time anyone had ever prayed for her in all of her ninety-one years. I was kneeling in front of a door covered only by a curtain. I got up, and when I moved away from the curtain, it parted and a beautiful woman in her thirties came through it. Never in my life had I felt the presence of evil as I felt then.

99

She said, "I am Susan, a nightclub singer. I want to show you something." When she left the room, I told Janet to invite her to church but to get me out of there right away. But Susan came back into the room with her arms loaded with pictures of her in different costumes. We looked through some of them politely, and then Janet invited Susan to church. Susan misunderstood and said, "Oh, I can't sing at your church. I don't know one Christian song." Janet and I left.

When we were outside, we both were laughing. Couldn't you just see the pastor's face if we brought an unsaved cabaret singer to sing in his church?

The next day Janet and I were out again. I had promised a lady we would bring her a Bible that day. Janet said, "We only have fifteen minutes left before we go to the church for lunch. Shall we go back to this house?" I thought Janet was going to take me to the lady who wanted the Bible, but God uses our language differences to His advantage. Janet took me back to the nightclub singer's house. When I saw the house, I knew where we were. I prayed, "God, You take

100

over whatever happens in this house because I do not want to be here, but apparently this is where You want me."

The door opened and we were invited in. Susan came into the room and Janet talked with her, but Susan cut her off. "I don't want to talk with you," she said in Spanish. Susan pointed at me and said, "I want to ask you some questions." I replied, "Okay, what is your question?"

Janet gasped and said to me, "You don't speak Spanish! How did you understand her?"

I said, "I don't know, but I understand, so let us talk." Of course, I knew how it was possible that I understood her because it was a temporary gift from God.

Susan asked in Spanish, "Do people who have problems come to God or is it people who have no problems?"

I said, "Susan, everyone in the world has problems."

She became angry and said, "You, you, you are an American! What problems could you have? You have everything."

I replied, "Susan, when I was growing up, we had no water in our house. We had no electricity and we had no bathroom. My situation was not that different from your own. But you are right. Now, I do have a lot of things. But I left my husband in Texas, I left my children in Texas and I left all my things in Texas to come here to tell you about the love of Jesus Christ."

Susan replied, "So how much did they pay you to come here?"

I said, "They didn't pay me anything, I had to pay my own way here."

Susan turned to Janet and said, "I will listen to you now."

While Janet presented the plan of salvation to Susan, I prayed. Presently Janet said, "She wants to pray and to receive Christ as Savior but she wants you to lead her in the prayer." So I would say a phrase in English, Janet would repeat it in Spanish, and then Susan would repeat it until we were through the sinner's prayer. We then told Susan we would be starting a new house church that night. We gave her the address and invited her to come.

Janet and I went to the church for lunch, and of course we were very late, which is a serious "no-no". When a team doesn't show up, the rest of the group doesn't know where they might be, or if they are in trouble. But when I explained to them what had happened, the

Americans understood why we had stayed. The pastor put his arm around me and said, "No, sister, she did not accept the Lord. We have sent many people to her and she would not even listen." I told him to wait and watch for her to show up for church. He said, "We will both see."

When Janet and I left the church, it started pouring rain. We were drenched. That evening, even though it was still raining, many people showed up for church in a private home. The pastor came up to me and said, "Sister, it is 7:00 P.M. and we can't wait any longer for Susan to come." Just as he stood up and opened his Bible, we heard the most awful racket outside. The lady who owned the house opened the door and there was Susan outside sitting on a motorcycle, soaking wet. The pastor brought her in, pulled up two chairs knee to knee, and started reading the scriptures to Susan. Janet came over to me and interpreted. Every time he read a scripture, Susan would say, "They told me that already today." Finally, the pastor stood up and said, "Whatever it took for this team to come here was well worth it for this one soul. Susan wants to sing for us." I asked Janet, "How can she sing? She told us this morning she didn't know any Christian songs."

It seems that afternoon Susan had learned two Christian songs. She had a voice like an angel. I told her later, "God gave you that voice to sing for Him."

THE LETTER

Some time after I returned home, I received a letter from Susan. I was very excited, and took the letter to an upholstery shop owned by a Spanish lady. I asked her to translate for me. She said, "I can read it, but I cannot translate it into English." Her twenty year old daughter was there and said, "I cannot read Spanish, but I can translate it orally to English if my mother will read it." So this is how I learned what the letter said. Sometimes the mother would stop and ask if this made any sense to me. I told her it did and would explain everything to her after she finished reading the letter.

When she was through reading, I explained to her what had happened on the mission trip. She said, "I have gone to church all my life and have taken my children, but I don't have what you have and what the lady in the letter has." She did not receive Christ that day.

A few months later when I needed some upholstery work done, I went back to the Spanish lady's shop, but she had moved it. I drove about ten miles to the location of her new shop, but I could not find it. I had decided to give up and go home, but when I pulled in to a nearby drive way to turn around, the shop was right in front of me. I went inside where the Spanish owner was working. She said to me, "I know you, but I have never done any work for you. How do I know you?" I reminded her of the time she had read a letter for me. She said, "I am so glad you have come!" She went to the door of the shop, shut it, and put up her "closed" sign. She began to tell me a story about her son. He had fallen from a roof, was in serious condition and may not live. I asked her to let me pray for him. After our prayer, she said, "I want to receive Christ as my Savior. Will you show me how?" We prayed the sinner's prayer together. I thanked God for the letter from Susan. It had come all the way from another country and led to this American Hispanic lady accepting the Lord.

INTRIGUE

Our team flew into an unnamed country. We went through customs where they decided they would open our entire luggage. The customs officials took all of our Bibles and Christian literature except for one thing. I had some two by two inch Bible booklets that were pure scripture. The official asked me if these were for children, apparently not realizing what they were. I said, "Yes," so he gave them back to me.

When we went outside, there were no pastors waiting for us. We finally found transportation to our hotel. When we arrived at the hotel, there was a young man named Jack waiting for us. I had seen him the year before. He offered to be our interpreter and guide. David had called one of the pastors and was told they would not be working with us.

We went to our rooms, slept, and then woke up early the next morning to catch a flight across the country where we would be working. David again checked the itinerary the travel office had given him. We arrived at the airport in plenty of time only to find out the wrong flight time had been put on our itinerary. Our tickets were not valid, for there was only one flight a week back from the country to the city. David came to me and said, "Alene, what do you think we should do?"

I said, "David, whatever it takes. We came to work and we can't just sit around here for a week doing nothing." David said he had only $500 left, so he rented a van for $500 to take us cross country.

The young man named Jack went with us as our guest to interpret for us. When we got on the bus, Jack sat down beside me. He showed me a rainbow Bible and claimed he had colored the whole Bible. I said nothing. I mentioned the barren land we were traveling through and he started condemning the local government. I changed the subject. It didn't seem to matter what subject we were discussing, he would condemn the government. I felt like he was trying to get me to say something against the government. We were not on this trip to get into politics, and we knew better than to make any negative comments. I said, "I think I'll take a nap," so he left to sit with someone else. Several days later, I found out he had done the same thing with everyone he had spoken to.

The next day we met with the pastor's wife to decide what the schedule would be and the church where we were assigned to work. Jack argued with her about his assignment. David told Jack that this was her church and we would be obedient to her. Jack and David had been assigned as roommates, and that night Jack quietly got out of bed, dressed and disappeared. We never saw Jack again. David came to my room and told us what had happened. Jane and I looked at each other and laughed. David said, "You two already knew who he was. Women are so much more discerning than men."

We knew about Jack because of the circumstances. Jack had left with no money, no travel documents and no transportation back home. He couldn't have hitchhiked because there was little or no traffic that far into the country. The only way Jack could get home was his unseen "friends".

We worked all week with each of us having our own unique set of experiences. When it was time to fly back to the city, we arrived at the airport early because we could not afford to miss this flight, since there was not another one for another week. When we arrived at the airport, the pastors were there waiting for us. They explained that they

109

knew about Jack and were afraid. They said they had Bibles and would follow up on everyone who had accepted Jesus as Lord and Savior, and they would give each person a Bible.

HOW I KNEW GOD WANTED ME IN AFRICA

My phone rang. It was Mike Downey. He said, "Alene, we are going with the bunch to Africa to an unreached people group, the *M'Bami* people. We don't know what we will run into there, so I am only going to take two women with us. If you will go, it will be you and Jeannie."

I said, "Mike, Africa is probably the last place on Earth I want to go."

Mike replied, "I promise you will fall in love with the people and the country." I told mike I would have to pray about it and would call him later.

That afternoon my phone rang. It was Katherine Hildebrand, an elderly lady from our church. She said, "Alene, you have been on my mind all day. I decided I needed to call and see if there was something going on at your house." I told her about Mike's call. She started crying and said that for two years she had prayed God would raise up teams to go into the unreached people groups.

That night my phone rang. It was the lady who worked with the young girls of our church. She asked me when I was going on another mission trip. Her girls had made me one hundred witnessing bracelets.

The next morning the secretary of our church called. She said that a lady she had never seen before had walked in and given her a sizable check to be used for my next mission trip. I said, "Okay, Lord, I'm going to Africa."

An African Chief

BEAUTIFUL AFRICA – THE WITCH DOCTOR

We had finished our mission trip to Africa and were in the van heading to the city airport where we would fly back to the United States. We passed through this small town where a lot of people were gathered and a commotion was going on. We stopped our two vans to see what was happening. Mike and Nicolai, who was from the Ukraine, told us to stay in the vans while they found out what was going on.

It seems there was a witch doctor and about twenty of his henchmen in the town. The henchmen were dressed in a costume similar to our Spiderman costume, but made from a tan/orange burlap. The witch doctor's costume was the same, only he had a hairy fringe from head to toe. The henchmen had long bamboo sticks and were making everyone sit down in the presence of the witch doctor. I was leaning my head out the windows clapping my hands and saying, "Jesus, Jesus." One of the henchmen came over to the van and hit at my window with the bamboo pole. I jerked my head back just in time.

114

The witch doctor saw Mike and Nicolai. He ran to a car they were standing near and jumped on top. He then lay down on the roof on his back with his legs and arms thrashing in the air like a dying bug. Mike stood there with his arms raised, proclaiming Jesus Christ as Lord. Mike and Nicolai got back into our vans and drove a little further down the road and into a gas station. We thought it was all over, but the witch doctor wasn't through with us. When we left the gas station, on the road out of town there were all these people with the witch doctor and his henchmen. Two henchmen stood, one on each side of the road, with a rope stretched across our path. We laughed, wondering if they really thought that rope was going to stop our vans. But suddenly the driver slammed on his brakes and stopped. Mike asked him, "Why are you stopping?"

The driver explained that he lived among these people and he was afraid. Mike asked him if he would drive over the rope if Mike could get it down, and the driver said he would. Mike got out of the van. The witch doctor was going to leap upon our van as he had the car in town. He was in mid-air when Mike reached out and pushed the witch doctor on his shoulder. The witch doctor landed on the ground. The henchmen holding the rope were so surprised that they let their arms drop, and the rope hung about a foot off the ground. Mike jumped in the van and said, "Now will you drive across the rope?" and we did.

In the street on the right side of the bus we heard a man screaming, "Don't preach your Jesus to us!" On the left, a woman was yelling, "Drive on, drive on, Praise God!" In front of the van was an elderly woman who was jumping up and down praising God. The henchmen had nothing to say. An African preacher who was among all the people proclaimed that this story would be carried all throughout the mountains. The witch doctor would lose his power over the people because the white man's God was more powerful than the witch doctor.

Be strong and of good courage. Fear not,
nor be afraid for the Lord thy God is with
you. He will not fail you nor forsake you.
Deuteronomy 31:6

JADA AND THE WHEELCHAIR

When we were in Cameroon, Africa the first time, our team met a young girl who was crippled. There was no grass in the village, so Jada pulled herself through the red dirt with her arms. Jada's ankles and feet were deformed at birth.

The red dirt was terrible. You couldn't get it off your body or your clothes. It was like a stain. We left all of our white socks and white underclothes and some of our outer garments there when we returned home, because we knew we could never get them clean again. The people really needed the things we left behind, anyway.

When we arrived back in the United States, Jeannie went to her church and put a notice in the church bulletin. She told them a young crippled girl in Africa was in need of a wheelchair.

The next week a phone call came into that church in Dallas, Texas. The caller said, "I am not a member of your church. My family and I went into this restaurant on Sunday, and found a bulletin from your church had been left on the table. I had just bought a brand new wheelchair for my Mother, but she died two weeks later. I would like to donate this wheelchair to you."

117

Jeannie picked up the wheelchair from the man's home. The following year, Global Missions Fellowship shipped the wheelchair to Jada in Africa.

We all arrived in Cameroon, but the wheelchair did not. Jeannie went into a city to work while the water well team, Joel and I went into the bush. Jeannie asked about the wheelchair and the city pastor said he would check on it.

We arrived at the airport to fly back to the good ole' USA and there sat the wheelchair. The local pastor took it and put it in his car. We flew home.

About a month later, I received three pictures and a letter of thanks to Jeannie and the team for the wheelchair. Jada will never have to crawl in the dirt again. There are plenty of people in this village who would be delighted to push that wheelchair.

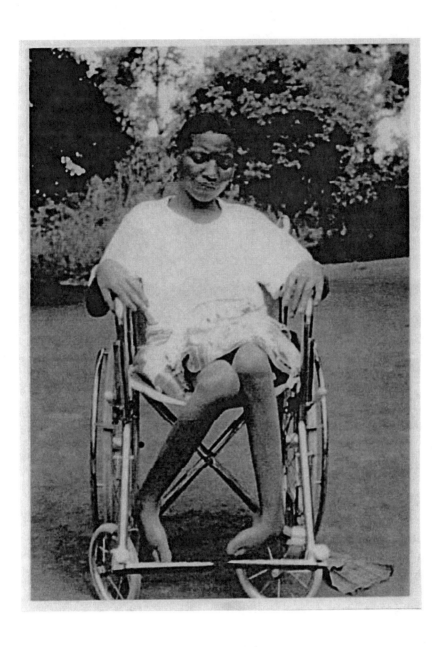

A LIFE SAVED IN AFRICA

When we arrived at our destination in Africa, we found we had to go to the tribal chief for permission to work there. The whole team went the first day. Mike talked to the chief explaining our mission. He then gave the plan of salvation and the chief accepted Jesus as his Savior. The chief said, "I will donate land for you to build a church." We were so excited.

Each team was assigned a direction to go witness each day, as well as nationals to interpret for them. My national was Jeremiah. We had to climb the mountain each morning and go to the chief first on behalf of the team. Then we crossed the mountains and looked for huts where the people lived.

One day Jeremiah suddenly stopped, so I asked him what was wrong. He said, "These are not M'Bami people. These are Fulani people. As an uninformed American, I asked, "So why can't we witness to them?" Jeremiah didn't speak the Fulani language. I would have sworn that there was nobody on that mountain but Jeremiah and I, but a man was standing nearby and said, "I will interpret for you." The three of us continued walking across the top of the mountain to the Fulani huts. When we arrived, we found a Muslim man with two wives. One wife was pregnant, and there were many children around along with one grandmother. We started witnessing. I would speak in English, Jeremiah would speak in M'Bami and the new man would repeat in Fulani. Obviously it took quite a while to witness since we were going through three languages. The Muslim man, one of his wives, the grandmother and two of the children accepted Jesus as their Savior.

When we were finished, the Muslim man said, "I have a sick boy. Would you pray for him?" He led us to a hut. I got on my hands and knees to get through the opening. "The door is very low to prevent wild animals from getting in the children's hut," he explained. When I was in the hut, there in the half-darkness I saw a fifteen year old boy lying on a bed. I saw an enormous bulge on his back, about the size of a watermelon. The back was so stretched that it was oozing fluid. I talked to him through the interpreter and prayed for him. I asked the boy's father what had happened to cause this. He had no idea.

Jeremiah and I went down the mountain for lunch. I went to our church planter leader, Mike Downey, and told him of finding the

Fulani people and the sick boy. Mike was excited about finding a second unreached people group, but he was concerned about the boy. Jeremiah, the new interpreter and I took Mike back to the Fulani hut. Mike stayed there and prayed for the boy all afternoon while Jeremiah and I went on to visit with other M'Bami people.

Mike asked permission from the father to take the boy into the nearest hospital. The man would not give us an answer. We later found out that this man was not his father but his uncle. The father was out in the plains area with all of the Fulani cattle. The uncle sent a runner out to get permission for us to take the boy into the nearest city hospital. It took three days, and we thought we were not going to be able to help the boy. The last day we were packing up our Land Rover when the grandmother came up. The sick boy's older brother had him on his back. We were excited.

The Land Rover was packed on top with luggage and a whole stalk of bananas. The spare tire on the back sported yet another stalk of bananas. We all piled in, all seventeen of us. We were packed in on top of each other. The sick boy sat on his brother's lap and my lap. I had to hold his back with my hands because he didn't have the strength to sit alone, and we couldn't let anything touch his back. We thought it was strange that the uncle had not come to see him off. As we drove, we again had to cross tribal lines, similar to crossing county or parish lines in the United States. Each time we crossed a tribal line, we had to stop, get everyone out of the bus and

ask permission to cross. Finally we came to the big chief of the whole area. Again, we stopped, and everyone but the sick boy, his older brother and I got out of the Land Rover. Suddenly, the uncle was at the window. He had walked most of the night to see the chief to tell him we were taking the boy to the hospital. The uncle talked to the boys in the Fulani language. I had no idea what he said, but he gave the older boy some coins. Then he reached out and took my hand. He just held it and looked straight into my eyes. I got the message loud and clear, "I am leaving these two boys in your care." If the sick boy had died, they would never see him again even to bury him.

Then everyone climbed back into the Land Rover laughing. The chief was so appreciative of our work and taking the boy that he gave us the highest honor that they can give to anyone – a live goat. The guys tied the goat onto the front of the Land Rover. We drove on down the road for awhile, and then stopped for a break. When the guys checked on the goat, they found it had slipped and was getting burned. They took it off the Land Rover, slit its throat and tied it on top with the stalk of bananas and luggage.

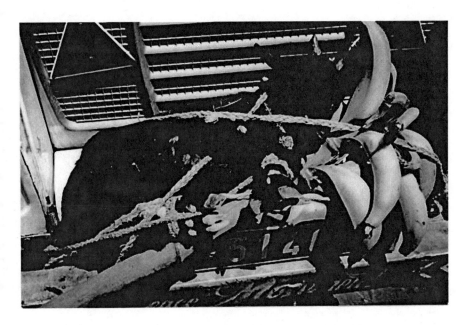

We arrived in the city and took the boy to the hospital. That was
the hardest thing I'd ever had to do. If it had not been for my husband
waiting for me to come home, I would have stayed there with the boy.
The child underwent an operation, recovered and both boys accepted
the Lord as Savior. They went to visit the pastor in town, and then
headed back to the bush to see their family. After that they left for the
city where they went to work. God blessed me greatly
on that trip.

INTERESTING PEOPLE OF THE AFRICAN

BUSH

In America, as a whole we believe in a monogamous marriage –
one man, one wife. The man who was our host in Africa had three
wives and twenty-four children living with him. The Muslim man had
two young wives when we were there, but obviously had had wives
who already died. He had fifty-one children in all, many who were
older than some of his wives. So what happens when you lead them to
the Lord and they understand the life they are leading is not according
to the Bible? They can't just dump their wives because they are
obligated to take care of them. I can't tell you the answer. Only God
knows. One man there suggested he only stay with his first wife but
financially support the other wives and children. This is not a decision
I should make. Perhaps God will give each man his own answer.

One day a man who worked on the water well asked me if I could

find some African walking sticks. Later when I was with the national

preacher, we encountered a man with a cane walking stick. I had

Joseph ask the man where we could buy several of them. He said they

did not make them in the village, that he had purchased it at the market

held in different villages. He offered to sell me his stick.

I said, "Oh no, I don't want to take yours!"

He assured me he would buy another one at the next market. We walked with him to his hut. It had a dirt floor, thatched roof and two rooms. We sat on small handmade stools, the only furniture in the room. Finally Joseph asked him if he was positive he wanted to sell his cane. The man told Joseph how many Cameroon franks he wanted for it. I gave the money to Joseph and he paid the man. The man gave the money to his wife. She came over to me, shook the money in front of me and laughed.

When we left, Joseph told me that I did well. "You gave him enough money to help his family and also buy another cane." I felt so bad, because in American money I had paid $3.25 for the cane. It was made of solid mahogany and had hand-carvings of pineapple topped by a metal tip. I gave it to my husband when I got home, and he is very proud of it.

The water well workers had a fit about it and wanted to buy it from me, but I wouldn't sell. The nationals told the workers that when they returned from the city, they would bring all three workers African canes. But when the nationals returned with the canes, it was all I could do to keep a straight face. The canes were the typical tourist canes. The handle was a very large man and the rest was plain. The guys were so disappointed, but were good sports, paid for the canes and never said a word to the nationals. However, they had plenty to say to me!

One day Joel called me over to the door. There stood many African women. They were honoring me because I had come back to the bush and I was the only white woman there. The African ladies sang and danced for me. It was wonderful and I appreciated it so much.

The first year Jeannie and I had to sit outside to put on make-up because there was no light in our hut. The wives of our host came every morning to watch us. We were their daily morning entertainment. Jeannie and I didn't mind and we became friends with them.

The first night we were there, our host's wives waited until they thought we were asleep, then walked through looking at us. We were spread all over the floor with air mattresses everywhere. I still haven't figured out how they could see us or where to walk since it was pitch black. We knew they were there, but each of us lay very quiet and still until the wives left. When they were gone, we cracked up laughing.

You meet interesting people and interesting things always happen on mission trips.

"NO MAN HATH GREATER LOVE THAN HE WHO LAYS DOWN HIS LIFE FOR HIS BROTHER"

When we arrived in the bush of Africa, we brought a cook and food with us since the people could not feed us. We also brought many five-gallon containers of water with us. On Wednesday Mike would have to go back into the city to preach at the seminary, so when the drivers came to pick him up, they brought us many more bottles of water. In the meantime, we realized these people had to go down a mountain to the river for their water. We only had water to wash our hands with twice in the whole time we were there. There was no water available to wash our hair or take a bath. Thank goodness for wet wipes!

Before Mike left, he called Robert and me aside. He said, "Alene, you found one extended Fulani family and where there is one, there must be more. Before you leave here, try to find them." Robert and I asked our interpreter about the Fulani.

"Oh! Yes, many more in the mountains." We asked how far.

"Not far." Now you must understand that we had no transportation since the Land Rover went back to the city. So we'd have to walk into the mountains. 'Not far' to an American is not the same as 'not far' to the M'Bami who walk constantly.

All of the Americans know that we don't go anywhere without a bottle of water with us because we can't drink the local water. Their bacteria are different from ours and would make us sick.

We started up the mountain about 11:00 A.M. and the African sun was hot. After a couple of hours, Robert came to me and said, "Alene, some of the nationals didn't bring water. May I share your bottle of water so two of the nationals can share mine?" All I had was a twenty ounce bottle of water. Robert and I shared, but we drank sparingly. Some of the others drank their whole bottle of water in the three and a half hours it took us to find the Fulani people. We were with the Fulani two hours sharing the gospel of Jesus Christ. Many accepted Jesus as Savior. Then we started back down the mountain. The afternoon heat was unbearable. We were all dehydrated. There were no trees, only scrub brush. Any time we could find shade, we would crawl under it and bring our body temperatures down. Finally two of the young American men came to us and said that they would take one national and go ahead to try and get help. They left us while we struggled on. My water bottle had about a teaspoon of water left. I kept looking at it but wouldn't drink that last sip. As long as I had it, I still had water and hope. I remember a conversation with my husband one time. While watching American western movies, I wondered why they would always throw away their empty canteens. Didn't they know that they would eventually find water and need that canteen to refill? Well, my experience showed me why they throw it away. That empty plastic water bottle felt like I was carrying five extra pounds.

We finally reached the village, and as long as we had been there, there had been nowhere to buy anything. But this particular day a little store was open that had Cokes and Big Orange drinks. God provides! The three young people had seen the store but had no money. They had walked another mile to where we were staying. They had rummaged through Robert's backpack and took some Cameroon franks. The cook had given them water and fresh orange slices. Then they had walked back the mile to the little store. They were waiting for us when we arrived at the village. They handed us

135

the fresh orange slices. I drank a Big Orange straight down, so they handed me a second one. The three young men had literally saved all of our lives.

When we got back to the United States, Mike called me and asked if I was okay. I told him I was fine and wondered why he was asking. It seems the two young American men were in the hospital seriously ill. He wanted to know if they had eaten or had drunk anything different than the rest of us. I told him that I far as I knew, we had all eaten and drunk the same things. Finally, after much questioning by the doctors and judging by the seriousness of their illnesses, the young men admitted that they had found a rock with water dripping from it. They had drunk from it. The young men did eventually get well. There is no way to adequately thank someone for risking his life to save yours. What a blessing they have waiting for them in Heaven!

A LETTER FROM CAMEROON

Hope you people had a safe journey. I prayed much for that.

Dear Mum,

It was a wonderful and nice stay with you people here in Cameroon. Your departure was not pleasing but I understand it was a must that you people had to leave. How is your health? After a long way gone and tedious work done in Cameroon. I hope every thing is fine as is my prayers.

Mum, I really want to thank God for you people. I want to appreciate your efforts in particular. Even though an age woman, you did not feel so tired of doing God's work. For true no man or woman is suppose to be tired in God's ministry. You did a marvelous job and I like it.

137

We are fine over here and the 15 year Fulani

boy is also fine. He was discharged and sent to

M'Bami clinic for dressing every day. Accept

my warm greetings and extend them to you

husband and childrend and grandchildrend. I

will to have a photograph of your husband and

your self. This is one of mine for you and your

family

.Thanks. Your In Christ

Gideon

MY FUNNY FRIEND

As you know, I went into the Bush of Africa, and on one trip the rest of the team went into a city. This is an incident that happened to my friend Ajay Torres.

We had gone back into the city the last day to meet up with our teammates, spend the night and fly out the next day for the USA.

Ajay said, "Alene, wouldn't you know it would happen to me! My luggage was lost and all I have had to wear all week are the clothes I came in. Fortunately I have on these pants that zip off so that one day I would wear them as long pants and the next day as shorts. The first day we were here, I walked upon this porch and stepped on a rotted board. I went all the way through and tore my pants here in front."

Ajay was going to show me the tear in the front of his pants, but couldn't find the hole. I started laughing and said, "Ajay, the hole is in the back."

He said, "Oh my gosh, I zipped them on backwards!"

Then he added, "That's not the worst of it. I knew I had to wash my socks every night, so I washed them, put one on the end of the hair dryer, then decided I needed to go to the bathroom. I flushed the

139

commode, turned on the hair dryer, and it blew the sock into the commode. I got down on my knees and had my hands in the commode trying to get my sock out. I couldn't let it go down the drain or I wouldn't have socks to wear the next day!"

I was laughing my head off. With Ajay there is never a dull moment.

In India, Ajay and I were not together but he told me this funny story. Ajay and his national had to cross a river. The only way across was by walking a log. The national did it all the time and had no problem, but how many of us could walk that log across the river? Well, Ajay didn't make it. He fell not just into the water but into the mud.

The national told him to take off his clothes so he could wash the mud out of them while Ajay got into the river and washed the mud off himself. Ajay told him that he couldn't take his clothes off because there were women washing their clothes nearby in the river. After some argument, Ajay saw no way out but to take off his clothes and let the national was them in the river.

Ajay forgot one minor detail – which underwear he had chosen to wear that morning. They were a tribute to America. So there he was standing in his brightly printed American underwear. He saluted and began singing "Oh say, can you see by the dawn's early light..."

Ajay has a great sense of humor and laughs about everything. I would be remiss if I didn't let you know that Ajay is an accomplished musician. He has played with the London Symphony orchestra among others.

I love going on mission trips with Ajay. When you are tired, dirty and just want a shower and bed, Ajay can liven you up. He makes you laugh, sing, and forget how tired you really are. He gives you the energy to keep on working for the Lord.

THE AVOCADO

One day Jeannie was out witnessing with her national Joseph. A man she had talked with had given her an avocado. She took it to the cook and told him how to make avocado dip. None of the rest of our team knew about this. When we got back late in the afternoon for dinner, there on the table was a bowl of guacamole dip. James said, "Boy, wouldn't it be great if we just had a can of Pringles." I laughed. As a matter of fact I had never before brought a can of Pringles on a mission trip, but I had this time. I went to get it out of my bag with James saying, "No way, I don't believe it!" We all laughed about how hard we were roughing it in the bush of Africa. We were thankful for our own personal cook who was wonderful and thankful for sitting there eating avocado dip with Pringles. No one would believe it.

CLEANLINESS

When we got out of the bush and into a hotel, Jeannie and I both took a shower and washed our hair. It felt so good to be clean, we thought. The next morning Jeannie said, "I know I took a shower before I went to bed, but I'm going to take another one." Suddenly I heard her scream, "NO, OH NO! I'll never be white again!" The red dust was still washing out of her hair and turning her skin red again. I was in the bedroom laughing.

THE WATER WELLS

I received a call from Global Missions Fellowship. It was from Joel. He said, "Alene, we are going back into Cameroon. This time the team will be in the city."

It just came out of my mouth, "I have to go back to the bush."

Joel said, "Alene, only myself and two water well men will be going into the bush. The rest of the team will be in the city."

I told him I had to go to the bush. Where was this coming from? I had not even thought about going back to Cameroon, but when he called, it just came out that I must go back to the bush. We hung up and Mike Downey immediately called me. He asked what was going on.

I said, "I don't know, Mike. I just know I have to go back to the bush."

Mike told me that since I felt so strongly about it, I could go, but I would be the only white woman there. I told him I didn't care as long as I could go.

The water well team, the four of us, left a few days before the city team. Joel was to fly into Houston and fly out to Africa with us. I had

146

never met the other two men, Joel described them to me. John was seventy and Mat was forty. I was to find them at the airport. Well, I couldn't find them, and I couldn't find Joel. I boarded the plane to Africa by myself. I thought, "Well, I may go to Africa by myself but the city pastor will meet me at the plane." Just as the crew began to shut the outer door, Joel walked into the cabin. He said that John and Mat were late getting there and the airline had given their seats away. Joel explained to the officials about our mission, so they put John and Mat in first class seats. We complained to our teammates about their luxuries, so Mat and John really rubbed it in with their steak and shrimp!

We landed in Cameroon. When the pastor saw me, he said, "You came back!" He shook my hand three different times and kept repeating, "You came back. Nobody ever comes back to work in the bush." He welcomed the three newcomers, and then we went to get our baggage. We had brought a computer with us as a gift to the pastor and to enable us to e-mail him to set up future mission trips. The customs people wanted us to pay for our own computer. We refused and went to the American consulate. They wrote a letter, which we took to the pastor's brother-in-law, who was a policeman.

After we delivered the letter, we left to pick up the water well equipment only to find it was still in the port city. It had not been shipped inland to us. We started looking for the pipes and mud we needed, but found that there was no drilling mud in Cameroon. After stopping at many places, one man sent us to an individual who might help us. The four of us got out of our van and told the man our story. He said, "There is no drilling mud you can buy in the country of Cameroon. How many sacks do you need?" He sent his workmen out to get the sacks we needed and loaded them into our van. The business owner said, "You are not planning to carry any water well equipment on that van." He called his workman over and told him to load the mud on the company truck. We asked him how much this would cost us because it would take three days to go across the country to pick up our equipment and get back into the bush. He said, "No charge. You are here to help my people. Just do right by my driver." Isn't it incredible how God works everything out!

We started cross country, arriving at the port the next morning. John and Mat went to get the water well equipment only to find that the officials wanted us to pay for it, too. After several hours of arguing, the supervisors went to lunch. The man who was left signed the release for the equipment in exchange for a small personal donation. We were finally on our way to the bush.

John and Mat starting drilling the water well in the village, and the whole village turned out to watch. This was the most exciting thing that had ever happened there. The water came in, the concrete was poured and the pump was set. John took a stick and scratched this scripture in the wet cement:

John 4: 3-14:

> *Everyone who drinks of this water shall thirst*
> *again. But whoever drinks of the water that I*
> *shall give him shall never thirst; but the water*
> *that I shall give him shall become in him a well*
> *of water springing up to Eternal life.*

The well came in so fast that John said we would have time to drill another one up by the new church. The only problem was that they were short one length of pipe. That could be taken care of – we would

go into the city and buy one length of pipe. This will be continued

into the following stories.

LEMONS FOR LEMONADE

As I had an injured foot from falling on the mountain, I was trying to limit my walking. That is a laugh when you are working with Africans who walk everywhere they go. One day I went out with Joseph. The American water well men had asked me to try and find lemons. Joseph and I walked and walked until we arrived at a house. Joseph told the man about the water well team and that we wanted lemons. The man told us to take all the lemons we wanted. So there we were in Africa picking lemons off a tree. We took the lemons back to our camp. The last day, the American men brought in the water well and used the water to make lemonade for all the African workers. They loved it and now had another way to use their lemons. Unfortunately, I wasn't there to see it because I had left earlier for the city. That is the next story – The Husband at Home.

152

THE HUSBAND AT HOME

Mat left for the city and had been gone for two days hunting pipe. When he returned, we all went out to meet Matt at the Land Rover. Matt said, "Alene, do you know a person named Kevin? You have a phone call at the hospital in town." I told him that Kevin was my son. My husband and I had an agreement. If we didn't hear from each other then we knew everything was okay. With this agreement, I didn't worry about home and could put all my efforts into the work of the Lord. If anything were to happen, we were to call. My husband had had a five heart bypass four years before, so my immediate thought was that he had died. I immediately went into my tent, changed into city clothes and slip-on shoes. I packed up everything into my suitcase, deflated my air mattress, took down my tent and put them both into my suitcase. With the time difference, I realized it was in the middle of the night at home. We had planned to use the Land Rover this one day because the water well men needed it the rest of the week. We had planned to drive into the mountains to try and locate more of the Fulani people.

153

Joel came to me and asked if I was ready to go into the city. I said, "Joel, it is the middle of the night in Houston and I won't be able to get a phone call through. I can't leave here without trying to find the Fulani and today is the day we have use of the Land Rover." Joel gathered the driver, the two interpreters and the two young city pastors and off we started into the mountains. After awhile, the driver stopped and said, "You can't see the house for the bush, but the house is just right there. I can't take the Land Rover any further so I will meet you on the other side." The other side of the house, right? Wrong! We visited with the people and some of them accepted the Lord Jesus as their Savior. We came out of the house and asked for the Land Rover. The interpreter pointed and said, "See those three mountains? The Land Rover is at the bottom of the third mountain." Joel, the two city pastors and I were stunned. We had to walk across three huge mountains. Remember, I had hurt my ankle and I had changed out of my hiking boots into city shoes, and I was wearing a skirt instead of slacks. One of the pastors left immediately and returned with a walking stick for me. I had learned how the B'ami and Fulani used them and I could not have made the hike through those mountains without it. Joel walked in front of me in case I fell on some of the rough downhill terrain. Each time we came to a Fulani hut we stopped, witnessed and rested. Then we would continue on until we arrived at the Land Rover. God blessed this hike because our stopping at the huts throughout the mountains resulted in fifty-four people praying to receive Christ as Savior. We also told them we were starting a new missions work in their mountains and had a preacher coming who spoke the Fulani language.

We arrived back at the village to find the men preparing to carry sacks of concrete up the mountain to the church site. I told Mat to put the concrete in the Land Rover because it wouldn't take long to haul everything up to the second water well site.

When the Land Rover was returned after its short haul, we loaded it with all the workmen who had built the church building, with two girls from Cameroon who had helped cook, with Joel and me and then we left for the city. I went immediately to the hospital, but the electricity was off, so we couldn't call out. I went to my room at the hospital guest house and lay down to rest my ankle. After several hours I returned to the hospital to call, but the electricity was still off. This time I was determined to sit there until it came back on. The young man who would make the call for me suggested I watch a certain light bulb hanging outside the building. When it came on, we could make the call. After waiting for two and a half hours, the bulb came on. I immediately called my son Kevin's house. My daughter-in-law Lucille told me that my husband had had a stroke and had spent three days in the hospital. He was now at home doing fine, so I called him. I had to confess to him that I had hurt my ankle. God had taken care of both of us. I had to go to the doctor but everything healed without leaving any permanent damage to my foot and ankle. My husband had no lasting effects from the stroke.

157

COCA COLA

The second time we were in the bush was with the water well team. I was the only American woman, and I had my air mattress and my tent. I always take Cokes and chocolate with me. One night I popped open a can of Coke in my tent, and Joel, who was outside, said, "Alene, what are you doing?"

I answered, "Nothing, Joel. What are you doing?"

The next night I was again in my tent and popped a can of Coke open. Joel who was outside said, "What are you doing, Alene?"

I said, "Why don't you come into my tent and see?"

So Joel, a twenty-six year old, and I, a sixty-two year old, were sitting there in a tent in the African bush drinking Cokes and eating chocolate together.

THE FIRE

Remember in an earlier story I told you how I felt I had to return to the bush again, and on that trip only Joel, John, Matt and I went while everyone else did a city mission trip. I felt there was a reason God wanted me there, but I didn't know what it was.

The Fulani family was there on the mountain in the M'Bami village area. I asked the pastor who spoke Fulani if he would go with me to see how the large family was and to see if the boy we had taken to the hospital was home yet. I had requested this trip several times from the pastor. All of the men wanted to see the water well drilled. Joel went to the pastor and said, "Alene really wants to go see that Fulani family and we can't go without you. Please take us." The pastor was not too eager, but he took Joel, me and a national up the mountain. When we arrived, the village was empty except for one little girl. The pastor questioned her and found that it was market day in another village and all the men and boys had gone. Only a few women and many small children were left in the Fulani village.

The little girl said that her mother was fighting a fire, so we asked

her to take us to her mother. There the mother was with a tiny baby

strapped to her back, trying to fight a huge fire by herself. The pastor

told her to get back from the fire, and the four of us started fighting the

fire. Joel stopped me and said, "Alene, you shouldn't be in this

danger. Here, take my video camera and start filming." I did the

filming. After a few hours, the three men had extinguished the fire.

We were told that a M'Bami man wanted the Fulani land, so he had

his workers dig trenches around the part of the land housing the

people, their huts and their animals. Then he had set fire inside the

trenches to burn them out.

Shortly after the fire was out and we were resting in the village, the woman said, "If God had not sent you, my children would have died in the fire."

The pastor said, "Yes."

The woman then said, "If God had not sent you, all my animals would have died."

Again the pastor answered, "Yes."

The pastor got up and came over to where I was resting. He said, "Sister, I owe you an apology. I did not realize God was working through you to get us to come up here and save all of these people from the fire."

I told him, "Pastor you do not owe me an apology. I did not realize either that God was using me for this purpose."

Now I knew why I felt so strongly that I had to return to the bush rather than going into the city.

RESTROOMS

We, as Americans, are very spoiled with all of our modern conveniences such as restrooms. I have seen so many different kinds as well as lack thereof. One time during our African trip, we were traveling in the bus when one of the ladies asked the driver to stop. We were in middle of no where, so the men were to take a restroom break on one side of the bus while the women went into the field on the other side behind some brush. When the women walked around the brush, there were some men with machetes cutting in a field. Of course the women returned to the bus laughing and said that we had to find another place. Mike was upset and promised the ladies that the bus would stop at a service station in town. We did make a service station stop, but when I came out of the restroom, I told Mike, "God's clean Earth is definitely preferable!" When he came out of the restroom, Mike agreed.

TODAY IS THE DAY OF YOUR SALVATION

We flew into Caracas and arrived at our hotel. The next morning we were assigned to teams and areas in which to work. One of the nationals requested that we go outside the city to a particular mountain where many people lived. Our contacts were a kind husband and wife. The only problem was that the wife was already a Christian, but the husband wanted no one to bother him. We could use his home as a meeting point for the missionaries and have lunch there daily, but our services would be elsewhere.

We went out each day and witnessed. The area was extremely poor. The houses had dirt floors and the children wore no clothes until they turned three years of age. After a few days, one of my teammates, Rosa, and I decided that if ever there were an occasion when we were alone with our hostess and her husband, we would try to witness to him. One day near the end of our week, Rosa and I realized it was just the four of us together. The man told us he had had a dream. Rosa asked him in Spanish about the dream. He said, "A voice said, 'You are mine. They cannot have you'." Rosa repeated it to me and told me she was frightened.

166

I said, "Rosa, will you just interpret for me?" She agreed. I asked him who he thought the voice came from.

He said, "When I dreamed this, I was awake and it has happened twice to me. I believe the voice was the Devil's."

I said, "Sir, today is the day of your salvation." Rosa and I knelt by his chair and asked him questions about his belief in God and in Jesus. He asked us questions which we answered.

I finally said, "Would you like to pray the sinner's prayer for your salvation?" He replied that he would and he prayed. His wife nearly leaped from her chair, and the two of them met in the center of the room hugging and crying for happiness in his salvation.

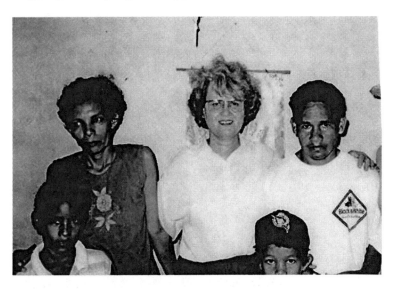

Each day we would go out witnessing, and each night we had services. One night we showed a film about Jesus. We were set up on an open lot for services, with our equipment plugged in to a house next to the lot with wires going through an open window. We realized that the people of that house had never been to a service, so we went to the owners and specifically invited them to the service. They said they had wondered why we had not invited them. We weren't aware that we should issue an invitation, but that is the way it is in the United States as well. Some Americans are just waiting for us to invite them to services.

The last evening all the teams, all the nationals who worked with us and all the new Christians came together. The event was overwhelming. Over a thousand people came together. The preacher for the night was a Venezuelan who had become an American citizen. He preached on the responsibility of Venezuelans to spread the word of God all across the country.

He said, "Who will come forward and agree to walk from city to city telling the story of Jesus?" The first person out of his seat literally ran to the preacher. It was our host who had received Christ after

Satan had told him that he belonged to Satan and that we could not have him. I sat and cried. Then an amazing thing happened. The whole body of people started moving forward. The only people left in their chairs were the Americans. It was obvious God's Holy Spirit was at work moving in the hearts of all the people.

THE VILLAGE – ROMANIA

We flew into Bucharest the year after Ceasescu was shot as he stood against a wall. A national pointed out the bullet holes in the walls of several buildings where the revolt had taken place. It was unusual for us to get this kind of information – the story he told us of the revolt. When we go into any country, we do not talk politics, we do not take sides, and we do not make any comments. If someone persists in talking politics we walk away. We are there only to spread the Gospel of the Lord Jesus Christ and for no other reason.

So many things happened on this trip in the village we visited. We arrived early evening. We just met the family who would be host and hostess to three Americans and our Romanian interpreter. We would live with them for about ten days.

During the first night it snowed. The morning was beautiful with the sun shining on the fresh snow. Birds were chirping outside our windows. After breakfast, we bundled up in boots and heavy coats and walked down the stairs and out the door. We had just reached the yard when we saw several Romanian women coming toward the house. They were weeping. The interpreter asked what was wrong. They told us their Eastern Orthodox priest had warned the congregation that if anyone let us into their homes, even though they did not accept our beliefs, he would not perform a funeral when they died. All of our visits in the village had been cancelled. What would we do now? I asked the interpreter to take us to a school, hospital or in to the village streets to witness. He refused. We could do nothing that day. That evening we had our church service and asked the interpreter to let us speak. He again refused. He informed me my head covering was not sufficient, and that the women should sit on one side and the men on the other side. We were in a small Baptist Church. Obviously each denomination is different, and particularly in other countries.

After the service was over, Matthew and his interpreter arrived from a nearby village. I ran to him, hugged him and said, "I'm so glad you came, but why are you here?"

He said, "I don't know. My interpreter told me at our service to hurry and come with her to your village. She said you are in trouble." He asked his interpreter how she knew.

She said, "I don't know, I just know they are." God reveals things to us and meets our needs. The two interpreters talked awhile. Matthew's interpreter convinced ours to take us into the streets the next day to witness, and then would take us to a home of a Christian. This Christian would invite her neighbors over. The following day our interpreter would then be sent into the city to work with Ralph

Edwards, my Sagemont Baptist Church missions pastor and a different interpreter who was not afraid would be sent to work with us.

That night at midnight there was a banging on the door. Johnny and his interpreter were there, arriving from another village. Johnny said, "We must talk with you three Americans in private." Johnny told us the Eastern Orthodox priest in his village had warned him that the priest in our village was an illiterate alcoholic and had ordered the three of us to be beaten. He wanted Johnny to warn us. The three of us agreed that we had come to serve the Lord and the Lord would take care of us. We would not be frightened off.

We went out onto the streets to witness. One man had accepted the Lord prayed to receive Christ and was going to fill out our information form but he had no place to write. He went inside an open building, so I began to follow in behind him. The interpreter took my arm and said, "No, you cannot go in there." I shook his hand off and said, "If you don't want to come in, fine. But I am going inside." It was a bar. There were several people inside drinking but none appeared drunk. The interpreter came in after me and interpreted for me as I began to witness. Three people in that bar accepted Christ as their Savior.

We left for lunch at the Christians' home and found fourteen neighbors inside. We ate lunch together. One of the men witnessed to the whole group. All fourteen prayed to receive Christ as Savior.

That evening at church services, the interpreter told me I might speak, but I could only tell them my name, where I was from and a little about my family. I did just that, and then said, "I know there are some of you here who don't want us, but we are not afraid of you." I told them about the family inviting us for lunch with fourteen neighbors there and all accepting the Lord. I told them there were many members of this very congregation who could do the same.

The third day we decided we needed to go see the mayor of the village and get his blessing on our work. We had a nice pair of leather gloves to present to him. We were trying to explain to him but he was not interested in listening to us. Suddenly there was a commotion outside the door, and then a large woman and a man came into the room. They were Christian musicians from the Ukraine. They had heard about our problems and had come to tell the mayor that our work was good.

The American man then presented the leather gloves we had brought

to the mayor. The mayor agreed we could witness. The two

Ukrainian musicians left and we never saw them again. Once more, God supplied our need.

The next morning our host took our interpreter into the city. Our new interpreter arrived and said, "I understand you want to go to a hospital to witness." Katy, along with our new interpreter, a national girl and I climbed into the car to go to the hospital in another city, leaving our American man in the village with a deacon of the church.

On the way there the interpreter stopped at a little store and bought two chocolate bars and then he stopped at an open market. We bought oranges and huge pretzels. There were no bags available, so the merchant took a piece of string and strung the pretzels. We carried

176

them back to the car laughing about our pretzel purchase. Katy and I

really didn't understand why we were doing this. We drove on to the

hospital. Our interpreter told us to wait in the car while he took both

the chocolate bars with him. He came back without the chocolate and

said we could go in and witness. We were taken to a ward. The floors

were bare concrete, the paint on the walls was peeling, and the beds

were rusted iron bedsteads. All that covered on each bed was two

sheets. There were sixteen beds in the ward.

We gave each patient an orange, and each patient broke a pretzel

off the string. The patients were thrilled especially since these were treats they never got. Our new interpreter was wonderful. He certainly knew what to do to help us minister.

We had an old vinyl record which had the story of Jesus and the plan of salvation recorded in Romanian. If you put a pencil in the middle and started turning the record, it played the message. The patients were listening when suddenly the door burst open. A nurse ordered us to leave. I put my finger to my lips, went to her, gently took her by the arm and led her over to the playing record. She was fascinated. She listened to the whole recording and then prayed to receive Christ. She left the room shortly only to return with two more nurses. She asked us to play the recording for them. Several nurses and patients received Christ that day. The nurse invited us to come to her home the next morning and witness to her two teenage children. Of course we said we would.

When we returned to the Romanian village a deacon came running out of the house, obviously very upset with us. It seems that after the last church service, many of the church people had decided to open their homes and bring in their neighbors for us to witness to. Unfortunately our time there was almost over and we weren't able to make all the homes. Katy and I went back to our room and took all the plastic bags we could gather up from the group. We filled the bags with the vinyl records, pamphlets, gifts…anything we could find, and took the bags to the group of deacons. We taught them how to use the record, went through our witnessing brochure with them, and explained the sinner's prayer. Then we separated, each going to a different home to witness. Many people accepted the Lord that day.

The next day we had to leave, but the deacons said they would finish visiting the homes and witnessing to the people who came. This was good, because rather than the Americans doing all the witnessing, it involved the deacons themselves to see how important it is for the people of the church to witness and to receive the joy that comes from leading someone to receive the Lord Jesus as Savior. They would know that person would no longer be condemned to hell but will go to Heaven because they were God's messenger. Before we left, one of the deacons had gone into the mountains to visit a family he knew. He was so excited that he had led several family members to the Lord. He vowed he would keep doing this because it was so exciting.

THE POLICE

Remember our first interpreter would not work for us so he was taken elsewhere. When our host drove our first interpreter into the city because he was afraid, something unusual happened.

Our host came home and wanted to talk to all of us. He said that they were in the city when a police car stopped them. The policeman had on a uniform and a badge. He asked for the papers, driver's license and other documents from our host. Our host didn't have everything required in Romania, so the policeman reached into the car and took out the car keys. Then he returned to his police car and drove off. Our host and the interpreter got out of the car and walked to the police station. They explained to the officers there what had happened, described the policeman, and gave them the badge number and license plate number of the patrol car. The officers at the police station said, "We have no such police officer, badge number or patrol car with that license number." Our host was stunned. He and the interpreter separated, and the host walked back to his car, hot wired it and drove home. He was concerned because the house keys were also on that key ring. There were no locksmiths in the village so the lock could not be changed until he went back into the city. Whose person do you think the fake policeman was? Satan works to stop the spread of the Gospel.

182

DO YOU BELIEVE GOD LOVES YOU?

When we start witnessing, whether in the United States or in a foreign country, we have no idea of the person's background and what we might come up against.

One day I was witnessing to a young man in a country overseas. He could speak English so I didn't need an interpreter. I asked him if he believed in God, and he replied no. I told him of God's creation and that the reason God had created us was so that we would have a relationship with God. I told him that God loved him just as his parents had loved him. He jumped up off the couch and started screaming at me, "God doesn't love me! My parents don't love me!" We found out that both of his parents were important business professionals and cared for their career more than their son. They had sent him to relatives at birth to be raised while they continued their careers.

We calmed him down and expressed our sorrow for his parents' lack of love. We explained to him God created us and would never turn His back on any of those who believed and accepted Jesus as Savior. He finally said he had always thought there must be a higher

power, but he hadn't known what. He said to us, "I believe in God."
We felt at that point he had endured enough and probably needed to
think. We left to return another day when he accepted Christ as
Savior.

When I was in another country, I was witnessing to a woman.
When I took out my Bible, she said, "I have never seen a Bible." We
talked a long time. She accepted Jesus and I gave her a Bible. She
lightly stroked the Bible, her most prized possession.

I left her feeling very sad. How could we in the USA have
churches everywhere, Christian bookstores everywhere? Everyone in
the United States could hear or read the word of God, but so many turn
their backs on God. In many countries around the world they have
never seen a Bible, never heard the word of God, and yet they are
hungry to hear. That is why we go.

> ***And Jesus came up and spoke to them saying, "All***
> ***authority has been given to me in heaven and on Earth. Go***
> ***therefore and make disciples of all the nations, baptizing***
> ***them in the name of the Father, and the Son, and of the Holy***
> ***Spirit; teaching them to observe all that I have commanded***

you, and lo, I am with you always, even to the end of the

age." Matthew 28: 18-20

THE PREACHER'S WIFE

Do you take for granted that everyone in your church, your family members or your neighbors are saved and are going to Heaven? This story may change your mind.

We were in Belarus and were assigned to a certain preacher and his church. We would eat all of our meals at his apartment. The preacher's wife cooked our lunch and then we all left to go witnessing. Judy and I were on different teams with different interpreters. One day Judy and her interpreter came to where I was working, saying they needed to talk with me privately. After the three of us stepped away from the others, Judy told me her interpreter had reported to her that the preacher's wife was not saved. This was a shock. It would never have occurred to me. I told my interpreter that he was free for the rest of the day. Then Judy, her interpreter and I headed back to the apartment. Fortunately the preacher's wife spoke English. The interpreter started talking to her first. She replied with some remarks about the rules of being a Christian, such as allowing no make-up or having to wear your head covered. Judy started to reply to her, but I stopped her. I quietly said to Judy, "She is not rejecting the Lord; she is rejecting her husband and his man-made rules." As I started talking to the preacher's wife about her husband, she broke down and started crying. We all three talked with her, and she finally prayed to receive Christ.

Judy, the interpreter and I went on over to the church because we knew the pastor would be there. I sat down by him and said, "Pastor, we just came from your apartment and had a nice visit with your wife. Pastor, I wear make-up, so do you think it has affected my witness?"

"Well, no," he replied. I mentioned other things and he agreed that they had nothing to do with my salvation or witnessing. The preacher's wife walked into the church about that time. They talked privately while she told him she had accepted the Lord.

I went to one of our American men and told him that the pastor had

a problem with man-made laws for his church. I felt that a discussion

with another man could help the pastor understand better than my

explanations. I never asked what they talked about, but the last

evening when all the teams, Christians from the churches and the new

believers came together, the preacher and his wife came down the aisle

after the service. They were arm in arm smiling. They came up to me

and said, "We want to thank you for **the** visit." I knew what they

meant when they emphasized the word "the". I thought, "Lord, You not only saved her, but You restored a marriage and a new team to lead his church." The Lord works in mysterious ways.

THE ILLITERATE LADY

We flew into Zambia and again were assigned nationals to work with us and a church we would work through. In Zambia most of the people speak English so I did not need an interpreter but I still needed the nationals to show me where to witness and for them to introduce me and get me in the door.

I was sent to a Nazarene Church to work. Our organization is non-denominational so we were required to work in many denominations. The Global Missions Fellowship just made sure the beliefs were basically the same as ours – one God, the Father, creator of Heaven and Earth and all therein; the Son, Jesus Christ, who was conceived by the Virgin Mary and came to die on the cross for our sins so that all who believed would be saved; the Holy Spirit which Jesus left with us to be our Comforter; the Bible as the God-given word of God.

Even though the Global Missions Fellowship pastors always checked out the existing pastors and taught the national pastors who would be leaders for the new missions, I was a little uncomfortable because I personally knew nothing of the beliefs of the Nazarene Church. I went to the local pastor and told him that I needed to know what his denomination believed. He gave me a small book to read on the Nazarene Church. To my surprise the first Nazarene Church was started in Texas. Their beliefs were basically the same as the Baptists. I would have no trouble working with this church.

This particular Sunday morning we started with a worship service. After that we planned to eat lunch with the pastor, followed by a meeting with all the nationals. While waiting in the church to go eat, the young people set up their drums, guitars and musical equipment. A girl in the back or the sanctuary started doing an African dance down the aisle. I went over to her, put my arm in hers and copied her steps. Now, I was old enough to be her grandmother. When we danced down to where the band was, we were called for lunch, so I left. Later during the meeting the pastor came up to me and said, "You did well. The young people loved it that a white woman would care enough about them to try their dance."

Zeta was assigned to me as national, and a couple of young men wanted to go with us. So day after day we walked more than a mile from the church to our witnessing area in a huge apartment complex. Many people came to know the Lord and were delighted to find out a new mission would be right across the street from their apartment complex.

One day as we were walking to the apartment complex, we saw four teenage boys across a field. When we walked back to the church later that afternoon, the boys called to us. We stopped and waited for them to come to us. They asked who we were and what we were doing. We explained and gave them the plan of salvation. When we first started, one of the young men walked away. The other three listened. Two of them accepted the Lord as their Savior and prayed the sinner's prayer. The fourth young man listened but refused to accept Jesus.

After a few days I thought it was time for Zeta to try witnessing. We needed to train the nationals to witness because it was their country, their people and their mission. They must continue the work after we left. Zeta refused. I couldn't understand why. She was excited about going with me to witness and about the new mission. She was faithful to her church. Three days before we left, I finally discovered that Zeta couldn't read. She carried her Bible and she knew her scripture well. I said to her, "Zeta, you don't have to use our literature. Just tell them what the Bible says and what God has done for you. You can lead them in the sinner's prayer if they accept the Lord." Zeta thought because she couldn't read she couldn't witness. Well, she proved that to be untrue. She led a number of people to the Lord.

The first night we had our service at the new mission site, only six people came besides the workers. However, the last evening there were over two hundred people attending the service. A new church was firmly planted.

A PROPER AFRICAN LADY

The people all over the world love it when you try speaking their language, eating their food, wearing their clothing and learn about their way of life. Zambia was no different. One day my group presented me with an African skirt. An African skirt is nothing but a length of material. They wrapped it on me over my own clothes, thank goodness. After that we left the church and walked down the city streets. Suddenly my skirt fell off and landed in the middle of the street. Everyone around was laughing and my team was in an uproar. Zeta laughed and told me she would fix my skirt. Then she explained that I had my feet together when they wrapped me at the church. She had me spread my feet apart then wrapped the skirt around my body. She said, "Now you will not pull it off when you walk!" They had done this on purpose as a joke on me. I laughed and told them I just wasn't a proper African lady.

PLANTING – WATERING – REAPING

Our mission trip was into Taiwan. Never in my wildest dreams would I have ever believed that this little country girl born in Illinois, grew up in Oklahoma, and now living in Texas would travel all over the world. Then why should I be surprised when God is still in charge. God can do anything, even sending me to Taiwan.

I was surprised when our team gathered at the first prayer breakfast. Most of our team was of Taiwanese descent. A Taiwanese church in Houston had sent in an entire team of workers. Unfortunately, few of them actually spoke the Taiwanese language, but it didn't matter, for most of the local people spoke English. They were a wonderful team. I enjoyed every minute I worked with them and every minute I spent in Taiwan.

One of the young Taiwanese men from Houston was my teammate. One day the preacher told him to go with another group. The preacher and his wife were taking me somewhere else. I had no idea where I was going. We started walking. The pastor said, "Alene, this lady we are taking you to see is my wife's best friend. Her friend will not let us witness to her. We have tried for many years." When we arrived at a small shop, the friend greeted us and took us to the stairs that led to the second floor. On the bottom step were slides to wear inside instead of your street shoes. After we changed shoes we went upstairs to the living area over the shop. The preacher introduced me as a friend from the United States. The lady was thrilled that an American had come to visit her home. The preacher asked her if I might witness to her. She said I could, so I started telling her about my family and about how important it was that we were all Christians. I told her the story of Jesus. Then I asked her if she would like to receive Him as her Savior. Tears were in her eyes and she immediately said, "Yes." I led her in the sinner's prayer. When we had completed the prayer, the preacher's wife was sobbing and hugging her friend who was also crying. The preacher wiped his eyes, but he was all smiles. There was such a sweet Spirit in that room.

The preacher said his wife had planted seeds and watered them for years and years. " I thought, "Why did God give me the privilege of reaping?"

Alene Dalley and Barbara Christianson are shown with a Taiwan movie star who gave up her movie career when she became a Christian.

The preacher and his wife

TAKING DOWN THE FALSE ALTARS

My teammate, the preacher's wife and I went to visit a lady who lived right around the corner from the church. We entered her home and were waiting for her two daughters to come home. One arrived while the other called to let her mother know she had a practice after school. Finally the preacher's wife started witnessing. The daughter went into her own room and shut the door. Her mother was very interested, however, and was eventually led in the sinner's prayer.

All three of us were sitting on the sofa. I was sitting on the end near an altar to a false god. I didn't say anything right away because the two women were talking. I thought, "How in the world are we going to get this false altar down?" The lady of the house looked straight at me and said, "I know I need to take the altar down, but I am afraid." How in the world did she know what I was thinking? The preacher's wife said, "Do not worry; we have a group of women who will come and take down the false altars and get rid of them. You won't have to do anything." The lady was relieved and so was I. These ladies from the church would not only take down the altar but would also follow up with her and her two daughters.

THE EVANGECUBE

We were in the bush of Africa. We had taken in Bibles written in the M'Bami language. When we started witnessing with the Bibles, we found that none of the people in the village could read. It is difficult to show them the Bible when they don't understand about books and reading. Our witnessing literature and our Bible studies literature was of no use to us. We found the Fulani tribe, but they didn't speak the M'Bami language so we even had a translation problem. Only one person with us spoke both M'Bami and Fulani.

Thank the Lord for the nationals who spoke the M'Bami language we took with us from the city. We were able to get people to listen because it was so unusual to see Americans in the bush. It was the first time some of them had even seen a white person or blonde hair. I went toward a little boy, who then ran screaming. I felt so badly about scaring him. Since the M'Bami people were curious about us, the nationals were able to witness to them. Over two hundred people accepted Jesus as their Savior.

After we arrived back into the United States, the young man who represented Global Missions Fellowship went to the debriefing meeting and explained what had happened concerning the Bibles and illiteracy. He said we really needed a visual aide that would transcend all nationalities, all cultures and those who could not read, young or old. They prayed over it.

Two weeks later another young staff member was in the office and said, "I have an idea." That idea was the "Evangecube". It is my belief that the idea for this came from God. The Evangecube was designed, manufactured and two years later it was all around the world.

If you haven't heard of the Evangecube, you can go to _evangecube.com_ on the internet, or go to Lifeway Book Store. There are several different sizes for clipping onto your jeans, carrying in your purse or pocket, or a larger size appropriate for witnessing to a group.

LITTLE HANDS

I was in a Trinity, Texas store one day. I had a small Evangecube on my key chain. While the clerk was checking out my purchases, I laid my keys upon the counter. The praying hands were visible and I saw a little hand reach out to touch them. I turned around and faced two teenaged girls and a preteen girl. I asked them if they would like to see my key chain. They said they would, so I told them to step out of line when the clerk was finished and I would show it to them.

We stepped over by the wall out of other people's way. I took out the Evangecube and went through the presentation with it. At the end when we ask them about their salvation, one girl said, "I have already accepted Jesus as my Savior and I have been baptized." The second teen told me the name of a girl who had witnessed to her two weeks before. She happened to be a girl from my church. The teen said that she had accepted Jesus as Savior but had not been baptized. The third girl said, "I have never accepted Jesus, but I want to now." I talked further with her to be sure she understood. Right then and there in that dollar store with other patrons watching, she bowed her head and prayed to receive Christ as Savior.

I took the names of the three girls and asked if they went to any church. The girl who had been saved but not yet baptized did attend a church where my friend's son was youth director. I called the church so they could do a follow up. The girl who had prayed in the dollar store was in the youth group at my church, so I called our youth director to do follow up.

God gives us many opportunities to witness. We just need to be aware and follow through for the Lord. People need the Lord. Many are searching, and there is no greater joy than leading someone to salvation and being a part of changing their eternity from hell to Heaven.

THE GRANDPARENTS – PERU

Our team flew into Lima, Peru and stayed at the airport to catch a flight to Iquitos. It was unbearably hot in the airport. We had to pick up our luggage, so some of us pulled out our air mattresses, sleeping bags or whatever. We took them outside. Then we gathered in a small group and put our things down side by side or head to toe and laid down to sleep. I laughed and said that my friends in Texas would never believe I had slept the night on the sidewalk. I would never do that in the United States. The teammates who stayed inside the airport were awake all night and woke us up in time to catch our flight.

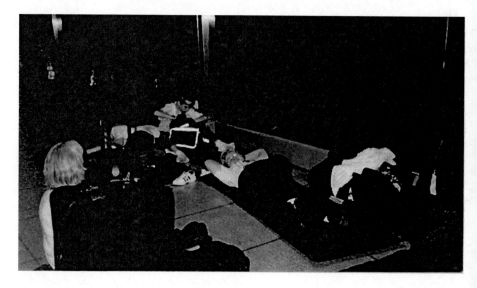

Normally we would have stayed in a hotel but the time between flights was not that long. We had to check in at the airport two hours ahead of our flight time as well, so there wasn't really time to travel to and from the airport and check into a hotel and get the sleep we needed.

We arrived in Iquitos and spent that day and night with the missionaries who would take us into the Amazon jungle. They were American missionaries who had a wonderful church complex. The church was large, with separate living quarters. There was a large open common room where we ate together and gathered for meetings. There were bedrooms upstairs and downstairs and could accommodate all of us.

The next day we left on the boat to travel up the Amazon to a village where we would work. Some Christians from other villages came to work with us. We also had interpreters from the church where we were staying with us. I was blessed, as I was given these two young men to train in our witnessing program. To me it was strange that I would train two young Peruvian village pastors in how to witness.

One day we were through but had to wait on some of the others.
Peter asked me to help him read my English Bible. There was no
place to sit so we just sat down on the grass. WRONG THING TO
DO! The chiggers were alive and well. The three of us had a great
week together, but we had others on our team also. There was a forty-
one year old man from Colorado along with the interpreter from
Iquitos.

One morning our team gathered. The interpreter was very excited
as he told us this story. His dad was a famous Peruvian race car

driver. He had crashed and was now in bad health. The son had gone to visit his Dad and told him he was going with people from his church to act as an interpreter in this village in the Amazon jungle. His dad told him there was another village eight miles from where he would be working. His dad said that he had been born there and was a toddler when his Auntie took him into the city. An "auntie" does not necessarily mean a real aunt, but could be a friend or baby sitter. After that he had never seen his parents again. We had gone into that village the previous evening and had a church service. The boy had asked around about his grandparents. He had an idea of where they lived and wanted us to go there. I asked the two young pastors who worked with me to take our witnessing territory, and I would go with the interpreter to find his grandparents. What a reunion! God always puts things together in ways we could not understand. Their two daughters were visiting them from California. Little did they know what was awaiting them in the Amazon jungle at their parents' home – salvation through Jesus Christ.

I told the interpreter that the two of us would go back and he could then spend some time with his family, but he must go through the witnessing with his new family. Five of his family members accepted the Lord that day.

When we left, the two aunts went back with us to the city to meet the brother they had not seen since he was a toddler. God works in mysterious ways.

THE PRISON

Our group flew into Belarus. Belarus was once a part of the Soviet Union. As our bus was passing a building, the driver told us, "If you look to your left you will see the old KGB headquarters. That is where your American man came." We knew who he was referring to, but no one said a word. We do not get into political discussions. We are there for the Lord, not for our government or politics.

One of our team members was Bob Gibson. Bob lives in Houston and runs the Lost Sheep Ministry. Bob is an ex-military man. He has a heart for the men and women who have served in the military and are now homeless. Bob operates Stand Down Houses which temporarily house ex-military personnel until they can get their lives back together. He also has a group of workers in Houston who go out to the homeless on Monday nights. They provide food, clothing and, of course, the Word of God.

This was Bob's first mission trip, but now he leads his own mission trips. He was excited, and asked one of the nationals if a military base was nearby. The national told him the largest in the country was there. Bob had the national dial the phone number for the base and tell the commander that an American man wanted to meet with him. The commander agreed, so Bob arranged to meet with him. It was not a military base, however, but a military prison. Bob set up a church service for the prisoners. Two of our ladies from Bob's team accompanied him to the prison. Each of the women gave her testimony, then they sang and Bob preached. When the service ended, Bob asked who would like to accept Jesus as Savior. It was incredible to see as the entire back row of prisoners stood, then the row in front of them. This continued all the way to the front. Over five hundred men accepted Christ. Bob told me that if the standing had started from the front, he would have thought they stood because the ones in front stood. Since acceptance started at the back of the room, the ones in front hadn't even realized what was going on.

On another day, the commander of the prison took Bob into the isolation cells. Bob talked with the men one at a time. A soldier from Croatia really affected Bob. He told Bob he had been fighting for the freedom of his country and had killed many men. Bob then told him of the greatest freedom fighter of all – Jesus Christ. The man accepted

Jesus as Savior. Even though he was physically in a prison in Belarus, he was finally free. Bob gave him a Bible.

THE FAMILY – KOSOVO

The ethnic war between the Serbs and Albanians in Kosovo had been stopped by UN intervention. The Italian peace-keeping force was there. Anyone could go in or out of Kosovo without going through checkpoints.

When we arrived, the International Mission Board had just rented a two story building and had a young American woman in charge. They had only been there two weeks so they were not quite ready for the large group we brought.

The upstairs hallway split the second floor in two parts. There were three large bedrooms and one bathroom on each side. The women were on one side and the men were assigned the other side. We put air mattresses, sleeping bags or whatever else we had packed onto the concrete floor. There were seventeen women and one bathroom. I know what you readers might be thinking, but you are wrong! We worked out a system and never encountered a problem. We Christian women were there for the Lord so we decided we would not have a problem with one bathroom.

During the nights we could hear rifle fire in the distance. Each night tanks would roll right beneath the window where I slept on the floor.

My friend Jeannie and I would walk every morning over a mile to a warehouse where we would sort food and clothing. We would then hand the food and clothing out to people who would come for help. Many of their homes had been bombed and all they had was the clothes on their backs. Some of the teams worked in locations farther away and had to take the provisions by van or car. One day after Jeannie and I were through at the center, we walked to homes carrying boxes of food. We witnessed to the people about the Lord Jesus whenever we would get the opportunity.

We came upon the home of a single man. It was a large house so
he had taken in a family of seven who had lost their home and
belongings to a bomb. Fortunately no one in the family had been
home when the bomb hit, so the family was intact. They were very
appreciative of the food we brought. They had no clothes except what
they were wearing, so we wrote down their ages and sizes. We told
them we would find them clothes and would come back the next day
bringing clothing and more food as well.

The next day Jeannie, Nancy Reeves and I walked back to that
house. The single man who owned the home was there along with five
of the family members who lived with him. Mona, the grandmother,

was crying. We sat down, I took her hand and we just listened as she told their story of the bombings, the fear and finally finding this safe haven. She finished by voicing hate of the Serbs and wanting revenge. At that time I patted her hand and said, "Mona, you and your family have gone through a terrible time. I can't know just how you are feeling, but in the Bible it says 'vengeance is mine saith the Lord'." Then I explained to her about God and how He sent His son Jesus to die on the cross for our sins. As I talked to all of them, the owner of the house would say, "What she says is true. I have read that." Then he went into his bedroom and returned with a Bible. Someone had given him the Bible a few weeks before. He had read some but had not talked to anyone about it. After talking and explaining more about salvation, we asked them if they would receive Christ as their Savior. They bowed their heads and prayed to receive Jesus Christ as Savior. There was a sweet spirit in that room. Mona thanked us for coming and told us that she now felt at peace inside. That night some of them came to where we were staying so they could view the Jesus film and learn more.

Our stay in Kosovo was an eye opener for me. I had never been in a war zone before. The Italian soldiers found out we were there and had sent a guard to watch our building. The soldiers didn't speak English but we tried talking to them. They did understand that we were thanking them. We saw a bombed out house with a beautiful pink rose vine climbing over the wreckage. This let us know that God was still in control.

ISRAEL

It was awesome to be in Israel and walk where Jesus walked. I had never had a desire to visit Israel but I knew I was supposed to go on this mission trip. Now I would give just about anything to be able to go back and have a Jewish tour guide tell me about the times of Jesus. We don't have the background and history that they have. We had a Jewish tour guide with us for one day in Jerusalem, and the conversations between the American preacher and the Jewish man were very enlightening. I believe that our Jewish tour guide was a Christian. He took us to a miniature scale model of Jerusalem, explained about the city to us and then took us into old Jerusalem. We went to the Wailing Wall and then to a church with perfect acoustics. We sang praises to God. We walked along the street where people used to bring their wares and sell them in stalls. We saw the church on the outside of the wall, the Mount of Olives, and the Garden of Gethsemane.

Jesus said He was coming in the Eastern sky, so outside of the Eastern gate of the old city, the Muslims have made a graveyard. I was told that the Jews would not go into the graveyard because it was unclean for them. The Muslims believe that putting the graveyard there will keep Jesus from going into the Eastern gate of the Old City. What they do not understand is that when Jesus comes for the rapture, the dead in Christ will rise. All will rise for the judgment. Nothing will keep Jesus out of the city of Jerusalem because it belongs to Jesus.

We worked in a church in Haifa. The pastor named Phillip and his family were wonderful. One evening the pastor took me and one of the young women from his church to witness to some Lebanese refugees. The man of the house told us about his escape to Jerusalem.

219

He showed us two wounds where he had been shot. The pastor witnessed to them and they accepted Jesus as Savior. Pastor Phillip told them to invite the other Lebanese refugees to his church and his church would help them.

On the walk to the Lebanese apartments, the young woman told me that Pastor Phillip was going to baptize her in the Jordan River the next day. I was commenting on what an experience that would be when Pastor Phillip turned around and asked me if I would like to be re-baptized in the Jordan River. The next day Jeannie and I were baptized in the Jordan River. It was an awesome experience. There were others there to be baptized, and we all sang praises to God.

One Sunday we were invited into a home where the couple held Sunday School for children. I make animal balloons and had little Bible booklets so we helped with the class. It was a wonderful time working with the children.

After the children left the lady told us this story. They had asked her mother to baby-sit their children. They had left their home and had walked only about two blocks when they heard an explosion. They turned around and rushed home to check on their children. They found the whole side of their apartment building was blown out. A car had been placed in a parking space by the building, and the bomber had blown himself and the car up.

Fortunately the grandmother had taken the children to the other side of the apartment to play with them before she put them to bed. There were no bedrooms left because they had been blown away. Many countries in our world live with the threat of bombings, civil war and guerilla warfare everyday of the people's lives.

THE MEN AT WORK – INDIA

India is a very interesting country. The Hindus worship mainly the cows but also worship all of nature. The cars must watch out for the cattle on the main streets. Pedestrians also have to watch where they step!

I was assigned a young woman as my national. Two others went with us by bus out of the city to housing additions. We each were assigned an area. When we went to the first group of homes we were to visit, my national spoke to a lady. The national came back to me and said, "I don't speak their dialect." The same thing happened at the second addition. Finally we saw a few scattered homes to visit, and found the national could speak with those people. It was a very unproductive day.

The next day started out the same way until I noticed a group of workmen upon a dirt platform. I said, "Let's go talk with them." The national said, "You cannot disturb people at work." I started climbing up the platform anyway. One of the men came over to me and wonder of wonders, he spoke English! A group of workers was just starting a coffee break so we sat down and talked. The English-speaking man was so receptive. He asked lots of questions. Eventually he and another worker accepted Jesus as Savior. I gave them each a Bible in their Language. I suggested to the English-speaking worker that he start a Bible study since there were about twenty men working with him. We left that area and finally found a wonderful place to witness the rest of the week.

The next day when we walked by the platform, I was so excited to see all the men gathered around my new Christian friend. He was reading the Bible to them. These men did not live in the area. They came in from all parts of the country and worked six months up to a year before going home. The Gospel would go back with them all

over India.

Many people accepted the Lord in the area we had found. They

were eager to hear. It is amazing how God goes before us and the

Holy Spirit has prepared the hearts of those to whom we are to speak.

I have walked past many people and would hand out one of my little

Bible booklets containing Bible scripture, but there would be someone

I felt like I must stop and talk to them.

The biggest problem I had while I was in India was with the food.

I have a little health problem and could not handle the curry. The first

day in India, the group ordered a platter of fried chicken thinking we

couldn't go wrong there. The chicken wasn't fried in a batter, but had a ruby red color from the curry. I finally found I could eat French fries and chow mein, which I lived on for the week. One of our men absolutely loved the Indian food and ate enough for both of us. He said he was going to miss it when he got back home until he could find an Indian restaurant.

MOUNTAINS OF GUATEMALA

Jerry called and said, "Alene, I know you like the hard adventurous trips so I wanted to see if you would like to go to Guatemala. We will be riding mules or horses up the mountain and staying with the Cakchiquel Indians." I had no idea what we would find in Guatemala, but I packed up my self-inflating air mattress and tent.

The group flew into Guatemala City and were met by a man from Mission Aviation Fellowship. He weighed each one of us with our luggage so he could put together the proper weight to fly us up to thirty-five hundred feet in the mountains. That was the location of a full-time missionary hospital. It took five trips in the plane for him to carry our whole team. We were in a single engine Cessna. I think it must have been World War I vintage. When I was

young, I received my single engine pilot's license, so they put me in

the front right seat. I had to wear the old leather cap with the

microphone inside. I could hear all the planes communicating with the

control tower. Inside the plane, conversation was impossible because

of all the noise. The pilot and I could talk to each other.

The mountains were so high that our plane had to circle in place to

get high enough to fly over the mountains. Then when we got there,

the pilot flew over the missionaries' house so they would know to run

the cows off the grass landing strip. With the rest of our team arriving

before us, there was so much noise they didn't hear our plane fly over.

When we got to the grass strip, there was a cow grazing, so we had to dodge her.

We walked to the missionaries' house and spent the night on a concrete floor. The next day the nationals appeared with mules. We rode from our 3500 foot location to over ten thousand feet up the mountain over sometimes wide and sometimes narrow track.

When our team arrived at the Guatemalan's house, we found our accommodations were not what we had been expecting. We had been told there would be a room for me and a separate room for the men. The house only had a kitchen which was half indoors and half outdoors. It had one bedroom for the children and one bedroom for the husband and wife. That was the entire house. The family moved their children into their bedroom and showed us the children's bedroom. When he showed us the room, he picked up some sacks and dumped them out onto the concrete floor. He was proud to show us that he had been out cutting pine boughs for our bed on the floor. The floor was concrete with a solid door to the outside. No windows were in the room. There was a single bed, which was offered to me by one of the men. I thanked him, but told him I had my own air mattress and tent. He took the bed and said it was as hard as a rock. One of the other guys slept outside on a bench, while the other one realized one of the other teams had taken his sleeping bag. He had nothing to sleep on except the pine boughs.

When I opened up my tent and put the air mattress inside with my luggage, I was in my own little cocoon drinking hot Coke and eating chocolate. The guys were envious. They gave me a hard time about my luxury and their hardships.

We thought we would be able to walk from house to house, but found that the homes were scattered throughout the mountains. We couldn't walk anywhere, so the next day they brought horses to us. Each day after that we rode to different places.

One day we rode to the school and gave a program for the children. My part was to make animal balloons and tell a story for each different animal. The stories were teaching morals. The teacher hung the balloons from the ceiling. That evening we showed the Jesus film at the school. We used a sheet for our screen and a battery hookup to run the VCR. After the program, as the Guatemalans walked through the mountains to their homes in the dark, they lit fire sticks. It was beautiful to see the lights dotting all over the mountains.

The next day we rode horses across the mountain range to get to a small church on the far side. That day I rode a small horse that had a short bouncy gait. The little mare also did not like to follow another horse. I have ridden horses very little in my life and that little horse and I had a battle until she found out I was in charge.

We were traveling along on a very narrow path when my horse slipped and rocks fell down the mountain. One of the guys said, "Hey, that's pretty scary, isn't it, Alene." I said it was, especially since it was my horse!

It was very hot, and we rode from daylight and arrived after dark. Once we crossed a stream. We let the horses drink. I dismounted, wet a towel in the stream and put it around my neck. It was soaking wet but it sure felt great in that heat.

We ate dinner then had to ride a short distance in the dark to the location where we would show the Jesus film. This time I was given a huge stallion to ride. I wasn't sure I could handle him. He had a long smooth gait, was sure-footed in the dark and knew exactly where he was to go. I was wishing I'd had him all day!

231

That night we slept in the church. Again, I put out my air mattress. We all slept in our clothes and since it was for only one night, I didn't put up my tent. I went to sleep, but woke up during the night to find a Guatemalan Indian woman and her small child sitting at my head watching me sleep. It startled me, but they were just curious and soon left.

The next day we rode down the mountain returning to the missionaries' house. Again we slept on their concrete floor. The next day we started ferrying back to Guatemala city in the Cessna airplane.

We went into the terminal to catch our flight back to the United States. Our flight had been cancelled due to a mechanical problem. We had to wait on a flight coming in, so when we finally boarded there were the people already on the plane, the people from our cancelled flight, and the people who had tickets for this flight. After we all boarded, the 747 took off. The pilot's voice came on the speaker and said that due to the weight load of extra people, the plane could not take on fuel. The fuel weight would prevent the plane from crossing the high mountain. After we passed the mountain, the plane landed on a short airstrip. The plane taxied down the strip, came to the end of it and quickly made a 180 degree turn heading back up the airstrip. Never in all my flying days have I ever experienced this. The only thing that was there was a fuel truck which refueled our plane. We took off again for the good old USA.

RICE

When we were in Guatemala at the home of the Indians, they were to feed us. We took rice fortified with vitamins with us. The Indians spread the rice out every morning and took all the vitamins out. When it was explained to them that vitamins were good, they said no, it was bad. We had rice, beans and corn tortillas for breakfast, lunch and dinner for a week.

One day when it was a child's birthday, they celebrated by killing a chicken. They killed one chicken and boiled it to feed twenty people. One of the guys had a box of Twinkies. I suggested he use it as a birthday cake. He gave them to the lady and explained what they were for. We never saw those Twinkies again! About two years later he came to a funeral in the town where I had lived. I was also at the funeral. He introduced me to his wife as the lady who gave his Twinkies away.

THE WITNESSING BRACELET – USA

I was on my way to the airport but I needed to stop at a craft shop and pick up some leather to make witnessing bracelets. These bracelets are made with colored beads:

Black is for sin.

Red is for the blood of Jesus.

White washes us as white as snow.

Green is for growing in the knowledge of the Lord.

Yellow is for the Heavenly streets of gold.

I couldn't find the rolls of the leather so I asked a sales lady to help me. She couldn't understand what I wanted, so I pulled out a witnessing bracelet. I asked her about her belief and her relationship with the Lord. She said her mother took her children to church but she didn't go. I asked her to step back into an aisle where there was no one else. I went through the plan of salvation using the bracelet. She said, "I would like to receive Jesus as my Savior." Right there in the aisle of the craft shop where she worked she prayed to receive Jesus. We never know when God will put someone in our path. We need to be aware and willing whenever the time is right.

236

TOYS FOR TOTS

I was always taking things for children on my mission trips. I would always look for something different and inexpensive. One day my friend Nadyne Carlisle said, "Oh, I can make you some tops." She took long dowel sticks and cut them to the right length then put them in the pencil sharpener. Nadyne then bought wheels to make little cars. She put the cut dowel sticks through the wheel, and then painted them bright colors. The children all over the world loved them.

THE BEAR

A friend of mine, Betty Walden, wrote the following article. I had the privilege of participating in taking the bear to India and helping to teach the class about different cultures and different places in the world.

A little bear in a tiny back pack traveled to many places. BENJAMIN BEAR belonged to a kindergarten class in New York State. In his little back pack was a small journal, a camera and a couple of small souvenirs. There was a list of instructions about the program with an address for sending pictures to the class while Benjamin was traveling.

While working in Alaska as a volunteer in the computer room for the Iditarod Sled Dog Races, I met Annie Myers. She had taken Benjamin Bear to the Iditarod from her daughter Martha's pre-kindergarten class at St. Peter's Regional School in Liberty, New York. Benjamin got autographs and photos with some of the mushers with their sleds and the dog teams. When I heard this story, the school teacher in me leapt forward. I appeared so interested that Annie asked me if I'd like to take Benjamin along with me to Texas. During the two months I had him, Benjamin accompanied Alene Dalley on a mission trip to India.

I found myself running out of time, and to get Benjamin home before the end of school, I flew to New York with him and returned him in person to the class. Getting to share my experiences with the children was exciting.

Isn't it wonderful to have such an innovative teacher! These children are blessed with a teacher who is truly interested in teaching. They learned great lessons about people around the world through Benjamin Bear.

MISSION TOOLS

- Bibles in the native language

- Evangecube

- Bible booklets

- Tracts – questions, answers and the Sinner's Prayer

- Evangelism Bracelet

- Colored squares

    red – represents blood

    Black – represents sin

    White – blood washes us white as snow

    Blue – the Holy Spirit

    Green – growth in knowledge of God

- Animal balloons – used with Bible stories for each one

- Story telling – Bible stories

There is a wonderful company in Fort Worth, Texas named "Sowers of Seeds". I have sent or taken their Bible booklets all over the world. I find that people have respect for a book of any kind. They may throw down a piece of paper, but they will read the book.

MISSIONARY DO'S AND DON'TS

- Don't be an ugly American. You are in their country. Have respect for their customs. Do not offend.

- Eat whatever is put before you and be thankful for it. Do not offend your host. The exception is that you should not eat or drink what you have been told not to eat or drink.

- Make friends with your nationals. Take small gifts for them to present at the end of the last day. They are your security, your witnessing ability and your transportation.

- Dress appropriately wearing casual clothes for every day witnessing. You may wear nice clothes for church service but not expensive. Wear comfortable shoes at all times – no high heels. Women should wear pants or dresses, according to the country's customs.

- Do not wear diamond jewelry or expensive jewelry.

- Wear a security belt under your clothes to carry:

  American money

Passport and/or visa

Driver's license

Credit card

- Do have on hand a small amount of money in the local currency. Carry a copy of your passport in a fanny pack, back pack or a light carry-bag.

- Never set your bag down. It will disappear along with your camera.

- If your plate is wet, dry it off.

- Do not drink the water.

- Do not use the ice.

- Do not eat anything that is not cooked – no sushi!

- Do not eat anything that can't be peeled – no strawberries.

- Do not go off by yourself. At work, stay with your national. On your day off, you must go in pairs or in groups.

- Take with you a card or matchbook from the hotel.

- Keep good records of names, addresses or phone numbers of the people you witness to.

- If you sing or play a musical instrument, do so. The nationals will love it, especially if you can sing in their language.
- Be sure to take your medications in the original bottles.
- I have never been sick on a mission trip because I obey the rules of eating and drinking.
- Take hand sanitizer to use before eating.
- Be sure to get any shots that might be required for the country you will be visiting.
- Be sure you have a current tetanus shot for the trip.
- Relax, enjoy, and remember you are only there for a few days. With God's help you can handle anything that comes your way. Remember you are the reflection, eyes, voice, hands and feet of the Lord, and you are there in His service.

MESSAGE FROM THE AUTHOR

I hope you have enjoyed <u>Joy and Adventure In His Service</u>. I enjoyed every minute that I lived it and writing brought it all back to me as if I were living it all over again. Anyone can go on a mission trip. You just have to step out of your comfort zone and be willing to serve God however God wants. One of the missionaries on the trip was a man who was eighty-five years old. We are never too old nor too young to serve the Lord.

There are seasons for all things and God gave me many years as a short term missionary, but that door was closed when my husband became so ill. After that I kept hearing in my mind the word "book". I didn't think I could write a book, but God kept putting that word "book" in my mind. People in my path would say, "Alene, you should write a book about your mission trips." Finally, one day a lady of another church said, "Alene, God has done everything but hit you over the head to tell you to write a book."

<u>Joy and Adventure in His Service</u> is the result. My hope and prayer is that because of this book, people like you who are reading this will

decide to go on a mission trip. My hope and prayer is that because of

this book, many people will come to know Jesus Christ as Savior.

- Alene Dalley

If you were to go before God's Throne and God asked why He should let you in Heaven, what would you say?

Romans 3:23: "All have sinned and fall short of the Glory of God."

Romans 6:23: "The wages of sin is death."

John 3:16: "For God so loved the world He gave His only begotten Son, that whosoever believeth in Him will not perish but have everlasting life."

Ephesians 2: 8-9: "For by grace you have been saved through faith, and that not of yourselves, it is the gift of God; not as a result of work, that none should boast."

Revelation 3:20: "Jesus says 'I stand at the door and knock; if anyone hears my voice and opens the door I will come into him.' "

John 5:24: "Truly, truly, I say to you he who hears My Word, and believes Him who sent Me, has eternal life, and does not come into judgment but has passed out of death into life."

The answer to the first Question is JESUS CHRIST.

Right now, trust in Christ with all your heart and pray something like this…

Dear God, Thank you for loving me. I am sorry for my sins. I believe your Son, Jesus, died on the cross for my sins and was raised from the dead. I ask Jesus to come into my heart and be the Lord of my life. Thank you for saving me and giving to me your gift of eternal life. In Jesus' name I pray. AMEN

It isn't the words that save you but the faith in Christ. Contact the church of your choice and follow up on your decision to walk with Christ.

Trust in the Lord with all thine heart; and lean not unto thine own understanding. In all thy ways acknowledge him and he shall direct thy paths. Proverbs 3:5-6

CPSIA information can be obtained
at www.ICGtesting.com
Printed in the USA
FFOW03n1851011117
41747FF

9 781438 950273